THE ART
OF TEAM
COMMUNICATION

Why team communication
breaks down and what to
do about it

DON ROSSMOORE

ISBN: 9798367060201

Printed in the United States of America

To Chris Argyris (1923 – 2013)

(Emeritus, James Bryant Conant Professor of Organization and Education, Harvard University)

He saw deep truths, that few others saw. He taught me right action, and how to learn. He gave me the chance of my lifetime.

CONTENTS

ACKNOWLEDGEMENTS

I am not responsible for this small book. Steven Wilmott is. It was his idea. He knew how to write a book and I did not. He has been an excellent project leader from the start. I am extremely grateful to him. Working with Steve is a gift. Many attest to this.

I am very grateful to Chris Argyris for his courage in demonstrating the ubiquity of defensive behavior and thinking in all organizations populated with bipeds who have cerebral cortexes. The honesty and insightfulness with which he and Donald A. Schon constructed their normative Model II gave me the foundation for interpersonal behavior that I had been searching for. Right away I discovered how powerful Model II was. I also discovered, over time, how challenging it is to master Model II under stress. The behaviors in this book are not Model II. The behaviors in this book are my own concoction that began with Model II.

I am grateful for the members of hundreds and hundreds of executive and management teams who used me well. There is nothing so satisfying as experiencing a team growing together by improving their communication and collaboration. Each time I finished a project and saw what the team was doing and accomplishing, I saw the limits of what I had to give. This kept me motivated to learn to

i

give more to each new client team.

I am indebted to the members of the "Palo Alto Study Group." With them, over four years, I saw clearly what kinds of practices produce new behavior consistently under high stress.

Friends supported and encouraged my writing, once it started. My wife, Marilyn Zweifach, persevered in more readings that she would have liked, and she gave deep insightful feedback. Richard Thaler gave me more reads than he wanted and was constantly supportive. Helaine Golann, Joyce Ranney, Rosely Traube, Joel Packer, Suzanne Dyer Wise, and Ari Nathan all read one draft or another. Each offered something that is in the book. Each gave me wonderful encouragement.

I am also grateful to Kia Penso who did a wonderful thorough edit, to Nora Ketter for a very insightful read and edit, and to Tonia Nazzaro for the book layout.

INTRODUCTION

On a warm June Friday in 1971, at a Harvard Square newsstand, I ran into a friend from grade school whom I had not seen for a decade. Jed Mannis was getting his MBA and LLD at Harvard, concurrently. I told him about my reading of Machiavelli and Clausewitz and the work I was doing with groups. Two weeks later, Jed sent me an academic paper that changed the course of my life.

For most of my life up until that point, I had been reading history, always fascinated by strategies and decisions in war and peace, the competition in the private sector, and the formation of corporations, especially in the industrial era. I played a lot of team sports and found myself thinking about team dynamics and leadership—subjects that are of great interest to me to this day. The paper Jed sent me was on organizational behavior, by a Yale professor named Chris Argyris, and at the time I had no idea that I could forge a lifetime career from these interests.

The paper described the normal and ubiquitous behavioral patterns in organizations that systematically create errors. These behavioral patterns are not conducive to solving the problems that teams want, and need, to solve. I think of these habits, as he described them, as defensive in nature, practiced without full awareness and understanding of what is happening. These patterns constrict, limit, and prevent communicating about the things that are most important to discuss. His description closely matched my experience of most teams I had been on and consulted to, as well as what I observed in my reading of history. It helped me shape my thinking about leadership, teams, and history.

But even more importantly he spelled out a methodology of how to help create lasting and meaningful change in these behavioral patterns that would lead to constructive decision making, planning, and implementation. Together, the theory and the methodology fall under what he called Action Science.

I looked Chris up. He had moved to Harvard. He gave me the opportunity to study and work with him for years. This became the foundation of my work with teams and organizations over the past 50 years. These organizations range from large manufacturing companies such as Hughes Aircraft Company, where I began my career, to a wide range of large and small organizations in fields including high tech, biotech, financial services, law, architecture, and political consulting.

Each of these organizations had its own communication challenges. Sometimes they were near total breakdown, sometimes they were doing well but wanted a lift to reach higher performance. Despite the diversity of problems these firms had, very often they were driven by key underlying causes:

- Persistent unawareness of its own defensiveness
- Undiscussable taboo issues that were damaging and being neither discussed nor managed
- Significant undetected variance between plan and action, at all levels
- The absence of competence, trust, and courage necessary to discuss the above problems productively.

A wide range of difficulties result from these causes, manifesting as uncomfortable conversations, stressful interactions, highly fraught interpersonal problems, frustration, and business failures.

The aim of this book is to provide a wide-ranging guide to communication in teams, including methods for improving communications immediately and over time. The book takes the form of a handbook that combines practical advice with a principled foundation for understanding why we communicate the way we do and how we can do it much, much better.

Above all, the aim is to help you get more out of communication, understand situations better, and experience more of the joys of great communication while avoiding the frustrations it can bring when it goes wrong!

We will start by looking at common communications failings and how to deal with them and then delve deeper into what creates these challenges in the first place, how to recognize challenging behaviors, and how to improve communication both as an individual and as a team.

The book is structured as follows:

- Part I: The highs and lows of communication
- Part II: Mastering the basics: Communication tools
- Part III: Communications culture and essential processes
- Part IV: Defensiveness and the roots of our communication behavior
- Part V: Mastery: A road paved with glass and gold
- Part VI: Conclusion: A lifelong journey

Each section of the book contains examples and discussion, as well as a section of practical advice for exploring the topic at hand. You will also notice recurring themes throughout the book that will come together in the later sections that deal with important root causes. Of these, defensiveness is the most important. It is accompanied by unawareness. Courage, compassion, trust, and a few of the other themes which ultimately are needed to overcome defensiveness, are also discussed with examples and practices.

Many years after meeting Jed randomly on Harvard Square, I told him the story of how he became my Angel First Class. He was astonished that he had done what he did, and wondered how he had had the intuition. And yet, with that one seemingly trivial act of insight and communication he had given me something immensely valuable.

This is part of the magic of communication: we often do so much in the moment that we are not aware of, yet it has lasting effects.

My hope is that this book can help you and your team get a great deal more out of the communications you have every day.

PART I

THE HIGHS AND LOWS OF COMMUNICATION

Communication is central to our humanity. Whether through the written word, a conversation, a wave, or the choice of where to sit at the meeting table, we communicate. Much of this communication is unconscious and hidden, even to the communicator. Getting communication right, deliberately or accidentally, can bring deep and meaningful results; whereas getting communication wrong can have very negative consequences.

In this section, we'll look at a few examples of these good and bad outcomes and what they might tell us about the causes. In the subsequent parts of the book, we'll discuss how.

Section 1: When things go wrong.

Section 2: When things go right.

Section 3: Our communication wiring runs deep

WHEN THINGS GO WRONG

One of my earliest clients was one of the first venture-funded data storage companies to go public. The company (we'll call them Harpers for now) was almost defeated by the common communications errors. The leadership team suffered a faulty assumption about working in teams.

The leadership team at the company was struggling with results; they had promised large revenue numbers for the coming year but were falling well short of their goal.

The chief marketing officer (CMO) had confidently proposed $30 million in sales for the first year after product launch. He talked confidently about the fact that there were plenty of prospects "inside the five-yard line." Each of the other three executives thought revenues would be no more than $16 million, and each faced a dilemma, "If I do not speak up, we may make a terrible mistake. If I do speak up, I will violate the team's cardinal rule."

This difficult situation was made more acute by the team's belief that the best teamwork came from letting each executive alone to do their own thing. Bad team dynamics, they believed, were caused by raising questions and doubts about another executive's bailiwick.

As a result, all three of the other executives had remained silent. The leadership team built the staff significantly.

There was no marketing plan at product launch. Privately, many voiced concern. Publicly, no one said anything. There was still no marketing plan after the first two quarters post product launch, very disappointing quarters. Revenues were half of what had been projected. Everyone was concerned with the CMO's drinking and his performance, highlighted by the continued absence of a marketing plan.

To complicate matters further, the CEO and the CMO had each gotten a divorce at the same time and became great drinking buddies. The CEO was reluctant to raise his concerns about his CMO's performance for fear it would cause the CMO more harm. What a dilemma: To help the company, the CEO must harm his buddy. To avoid harming his buddy, he must harm the company.

This is a true story, and it has a happy ending. Although the situation at the company may seem a little extreme, it is illustrative. Most teams hold some assumptions that are not true and are a source of problems that remain uncorrected. Every team produces issues that need to be managed better but remain undiscussed. While an issue is undiscussed, it cannot be productively managed. This is normal team behavior. It reliably produces errors.

When things go wrong in communication, they can range from mundane failures to dramatic heart-wrenching events. The foundational errors include:

- Every organization produces issues that need to be managed better yet are systematically avoided.

- The discussion of difficult issues tends to be high in judgment, attribution, and vagueness, while poor in data and inquiry.

- What individuals, groups, and organizations do differs from what they intend to do and from what they think they did. All remain unaware of the differences between intentions and actions. This lack of awareness increases the difficulty and lowers the likelihood of successful problem solving, decision making, and implementation.

- Decisions made behind closed doors create resistance in those outside the closed doors.

When communication goes wrong and stays wrong, trust, collaboration, and morale are often harmed. Worst of all, since communication itself is deteriorating or devalued, the very tool needed to fix the situation is under threat.

WHEN THINGS GO RIGHT

While working with Harpers, I met for a day with the executive team. After the CEO's introduction, the discussion went to the familiar topic of targets versus performance. The CMO talked confidently about the pipeline and prospects.

As fear rose of another trip around the same discussion, it was clear to everyone in the room that the issues that needed to be addressed were being suppressed by everybody. The chief of engineering expressed his concerns about the planned numbers, the chief financial officer (CFO) voiced similar sentiments. Finally, the executives decided to go into the field and visit the prospects, to see for themselves.

They came back from the field visits, compared notes, decided they were likely to do $16 million, and then trimmed almost 40 percent of their staff. The firsthand evidence was too compelling to ignore. It also provided a solid basis of facts for discussion, which allowed the group to have a full and frank discussion of the marketing area without the CMO controlling the debate.

The team also came to a new understanding that key issues could not be swept under the carpet. While they initially feared harm from opening a debate in each of their areas of specialty, they quickly found it was also very valuable. The discussions of difficult, high-stress issues were challenging but they led to leadership team members being able to share problems earlier and getting unbiased insights. There was still a respect for confidentiality, but discussions could often be more to the point than they could be with direct subordinates in each organization.

The new target market focus brought by the new CMO and these in-depth discussions were a large part of the company's subsequent success and IPO. It was the largest IPO in history, to that date.

It's tempting to think that everything problematic simply stemmed from a CMO who had challenges in his personal life and was unable to keep on top of his job. This is far from the truth, however. The lack of discussion denied the CMO the chance to see the harm he was doing, it enabled the CEO to allow the situation to go unaddressed, and it stifled debate about what the right strategy really was.

Communication can be a great joy, unlocking insights and empathy, and it can also be terribly painful. Both good and bad can happen with the same individuals in the room! As happened at Harpers, the right information, when it gets listened to, can have a huge impact. Getting opinions on the table that are not normally shared can dramatically change perspectives. Having participants see descriptive, valid information for themselves switches on lightbulbs.

Many of the most important breakthroughs happen in moments like these.

Great communication results in:

- **Feelings of new understanding**: Aha! moments when previously unconnected facts come together and someone in the room sees a connection that wasn't there before.

- **Feelings of *shared* understanding**: different parties in the communication coming to the same realization or one party explaining it to others so that new insight is gained. Like being let in on a group secret, shared understanding creates a feeling of group belonging that is hard to match.

- **The sparking of a great idea that rolls around the room getting better**: The continuation of an "Aha! moment" that not only becomes shared but gets improved upon with a rush of new ideas all flooding in as if a previously locked door had been opened.

- **The sharing of genuine empathy, connection, and compassion**: moments when it becomes clear that another understands an emotion or feeling and accepts, understands, or encourages it.

- **A clear decision**: periods in a conversation where options are assessed and discussed but ultimately a group consensus is reached on which option to pursue so that everyone can leave the discussion with a clear sense of purpose.

- **A shared experience**: moments when events, a view, music, or some other phenomenon is experienced by several people at the same time and shared understanding of facts or emotions occurs, even if there is no verbal communication.

All these and many other experiences show how intrinsic to the human experience good communication really is. A shared idea, a revelation, the feeling of having crafted something together—these make the heart jump.

OUR COMMUNICATIONS WIRING RUNS DEEP

A favorite early project was the integration of three systems labs. The company was a large multinational which we will call Halogen and was changing strategy. The company wanted to move from selling boxes filled with electronics, to selling networks of boxes filled with electronics. Each of the three major business units had its own operating system and systems lab. I was asked to help integrate the three labs. However, as I interviewed senior executives in each of the three business units, it became clear that they hated my client Ralph, the executive chosen to lead the integrated systems lab. They said things like, "I hope I never have to do business with him again."

This contrasted heavily with the opinion of everyone in the three systems labs who loved Ralph.

Ralph had earned his PhD from a top computer science program. The culture when Ralph was a student was that the person with the sharpest tongue won the argument. Ralph sometimes had a very sharp tongue. At times he used it like a stiletto. At other times he was kind, very funny, and empathic. He tried to influence the business unit executives with his stiletto instead of with his kind, funny empathy. They hated him for this. Ralph was unaware of the unintended consequences of his influence strategy.

This is a common pattern for many communicators, especially for those who have advanced to senior positions within an organization. Their personal style becomes familiar to them and, for all they know, is effective. However, it can often get wildly different reactions from different groups. These basic communications traits are present in every interaction and often quite unconscious.

I met Ralph and his team on the campus of the largest systems lab to begin the process of integration. The first slide I presented to the team was "What is working well." The next slide was, "What needs to work better." The first bullet on this slide said, "The BU execs hate Ralph." Karl, Ralph's best friend, who had reluctantly confirmed the opinions I had heard from the business unit executives, was sitting next to Ralph. He turned red, stared death daggers at me, pushed himself away from the table, and said, "F… you." Luckily, Ralph turned to his friend and said, "Come back to the table, Karl. This is important. We need to hear this."

Eventually, Ralph dramatically improved his relationships with the business unit executives, so much so that in the next budgeting cycle they gave him more money than he asked for; however, to get there took a major moment of realization and then the willingness to listen and work on the problem. Once he was aware, he worked hard at changing his influence strategy and succeeded, winning the trust and appreciation of the business unit executives.

Many patterns of communication are self-reinforcing. This often means negative patterns become deeply embedded in a team's communications culture and are very hard to undo. Not mentioning that a senior executive is an alcoholic becomes ingrained, not delivering bad news to the CEO becomes habitual, and not raising the difficult issues becomes the way. It takes moments of courage on the part of the participants like Ralph to step over these hurdles and reset the script.

As we will see in the following chapters, many communications patterns stem from behaviors driven by the three key errors:

1. A deep-rooted defensiveness that manifests itself in what we choose to communicate about, how we carry out that communication, and how we react to feedback

2. A shocking lack of awareness of how others are reacting to our communication

3. An erosion of trust in a team to the extent that communication is barely useful for addressing the real challenges faced by the team.

These behaviors make sense in some context (we are defensive for a reason), but if they run riot they are reinforced over and over again to create a wide array of problems.

It is extremely challenging for a group of people to build up enough awareness, compassion, and trust to be genuinely open in their communication. It takes courage to get there. As we will see, we are wired as human beings to take a defensive stance in many of our dealings with others: the fear of failing out of the group seems too great to let us do otherwise. We will also see, however, that there are ways of getting around our defensiveness once we know how much it influences us.

PART II

MASTERING THE BASICS: COMMUNICATION TOOLS

In the mid-1980's I was consulting for a well-known multinational company. In one of their key growing business units, the hardware team felt bullied by the software team, and the software team felt that the hardware team was ignoring their needs for the operating system. Product development had come to a halt. The teams decided to meet and have the conversation facilitated by an outsider.

Before the meeting started, the room was tense. Hardware was talking to Hardware and Software was talking to Software.

Then, Hardware offered to hear software's complaints, first. The head of hardware took the lead in summarizing what Software said. Other members of the Hardware team asked follow-up questions. Hardware inquired of each of the six Software members in the room. They asked for examples of Software experiencing Hardware not listening. Examples were offered and explored. People from Hardware summarized, inquired, and then apologized.

At the break, two people from Software were talking with two people from Hardware. Then Software asked to hear Hardware's complaints. They, too, summarized and inquired. They asked for examples of Software bullying and insulting Hardware. Examples, again, were offered and explored. Everyone from Software apologized and expressed regret.

At the end of the day, five of six people from each group were talking to folks from the other group. There was even a little laughter. Communication and collaboration improved enough that the product was delivered on time.

This illustrates the value of truly understanding what is being said. Listening is the basic communication competence that we will cover in this section. Others include summarizing, inquiring, advocating, and distinguishing facts and opinions.

In this second section of the book, we will cover these key communications tools. In almost every case, most people feel they are good at these basic competencies. However, on closer examination, this turns out to be far from the truth for most of us. There is no shame in this; instead, there is a world of opportunity ready to be unlocked by being conscious of these tools and using them more effectively.

The tools we will cover in this section are: Listening, summarizing, inquiring, advocating, coupling facts and opinions, and interrupting interruptions. These tools promote and support dialogue. Dialogue is essential to all teams. In the virtual world, interpersonal interaction is essential to holding participants' attention and engagement. Every section ends with practices.

LISTENING: DID YOU REALLY LISTEN?

Listening well is a powerful tool. It is also a great challenge. At first, it requires single-minded attention. From the time we begin developing language as young children, we hear voices in our heads. We talk to ourselves before we start talking with others. Talking to ourselves, or listening to the voices inside us, is a very early habit. It is deeply rooted. Our inner voices are captivating. We often confuse these voices with external voices, and we remain unaware that we are doing so. This is a fundamental source of miscommunication and mistrust.

What happens to us when someone else talks? Sometimes we do a running commentary on what we think is being said. Sometimes we are designing and rehearsing what we will say next. Sometimes we are thinking about things that are not even part of the conversation at hand. Over and over, when someone else is talking, we only partially listen to the person talking. When we listen to voices inside ourselves, what is said by others is obscured.

This listening with only one ear, or half-listening, is common. Indeed, it is, and always has been, normal. Most of the time we are half-listening; we are just unaware of it.

Our internal dialogues can be so compelling that we get lost in them, confusing them with the reality outside of our skin. Here are some common errors we fall into when half-listening:

- We lose focus on what the speaker is saying
- Even if we still hear the words, we are unlikely to glean sufficient meaning from them
- We miss how others in the room are reacting to what the speaker is saying.

All this may seem justifiable if the time is being spent mustering arguments for how to counter what is being said (or support it). Though this seems logical, it is self-defeating.

As soon as the listening stops and the preparation of arguments begins, we lose track of the conversation and thus are likely to deliver arguments that, at best, miss the mark. At worst, it makes it obvious we have not been listening. So often, during a meeting, each time someone talks, a new conversation is started.

This has become even worse in the virtual video conference age where the group video discussion is often just one window on the computer screen, with web links, emails, and other distractions just a click away.

Usually, when we half-listen, we assume we have heard and understood exactly as the speaker intended. We usually do not discover a misunderstanding until the conversation has veered off at a tangent or, worse still, work has begun on a task that is rooted in a misunderstanding.

To listen better begins with self-mindfulness. To become mindful of when we are half-listening, we must cultivate awareness-in-the-moment of when we are half-listening. How might we cultivate mindfulness of ourselves? To cultivate mindfulness in the moment of our half-listening, we can learn to monitor any of the following: cognition (What we are saying to ourselves/our inner voices), emotion (how we are feeling), behavior (interpersonal, verbatim) the musculoskeletal structure (posture and movement), and the autonomic nervous system (breath, pulse, heart rate, blood pressure). Learning to monitor any one of these many channels is necessary to monitor our half-listening.

It is important to find a small number of indicative behaviors to allow you to identify whether you are half-listening or fully listening. Are you able to take notes, are you aware of the facial expressions or posture of the other listeners, and so on? What can you do to discover and remove distractions?

Most of us would call ourselves "good listeners," but very often we either do not listen at all or we don't focus enough on the other person to truly understand. Most of us have no less than a few voices talking inside of us at the same time.

There ought to be a law, "When listening to someone else, no talking to yourself." Often as listeners, we transform vagueness and ambiguity into something clear that we either like or dislike.

An important milestone for every first-rate listener I know is the recognition that internal voices are not reality. The best listening is, in fact, a meditation. This can be hard to achieve in a meeting at first; the key point is that it requires focus to understand what is being said, what the speaker really means, and how others in the room perceive it. Attending to this is crucial to being effective when it does come time to speak.

All this leaves three key questions:

1. How do I get better at listening?
2. Given that I may need to speak, how do I find time to prepare my remarks?
3. How do I get others in the meeting to listen to me and to each other?

Questions 1 and 2 are challenging because many of us are conditioned to fall into precisely those traps explained here. Question 3 will be answered in the coming sections.

Question 1 (how to listen): When I began learning how to listen, I wrote down, word for word, what was said. This taught me to listen verbatim. Then I read my verbatims out loud. I discovered that my commitment to summarizing publicly (which is covered in the next section) motivated me to listen as well as I could. I stopped taking verbatim notes and just listened with my whole body.

Each of us has listening postures. We have a few postures that accompany our active, competent listening and a similar number of postures that accompany our half-listening. Practice putting on your half-listening body and then replacing it with your listening body. Do this over and over. Note, within you, points of most interesting sensation. Get to know these points. They will tell you what body you are in. This practice develops awareness of our listening by developing awareness of our bodies so we can recognize in the moment what listening we are doing. The face, the voice, the breath can be used in the same way to cultivate our listening awareness. Each form of listening is accompanied by a few faces, voices, and breaths. The more one practices, the more awareness is cultivated. I have found this a very worthwhile investment of my time, because my listening gets better and better. Listening makes everything easier.

Question 2 (how to prepare your own words whilst listening attentively): Trust that listening well is the best preparation for responding well; trust that your unconscious mind will do even a better job designing the right response than your conscious mind. The foundation of success here is to make sure you've understood what's been said before you make your point. The most powerful way to do this is with a summary. We will cover this in-depth in the next section but, in essence, the technique here is:

- Allow the speaker to finish,
- Begin your words by saying "Let me summarize what you just said,"
- Once your summary has been delivered, ask the speaker to correct anything you said,
- Then add your point of view to the mix.

Doing this shows you have a deep appreciation of what has already been said and creates a pause in which you formulate your own point in the context that has just been created. It is also a powerful way to determine whether you missed anything in what went before. Every team that has used summary has reduced communication errors and improved mutual respect and trust.

Most of the best listeners I know are still when they listen, but there are exceptions: An executive I had worked with in India, otherwise competent, was a terrible listener. Then we went hiking in the Western Ghat mountains. On steep and difficult terrain, he was nimble and graceful. He became a mountain goat. I saw how much he liked to move. Monday, back at the office, I suggested that instead of sitting during meetings, he roam around the room. When roaming he was an excellent listener, summarizing complex statements to the speakers' satisfaction. Another executive listened best when twirling a pen between his thumb and first finger.

There is no one ideal way to listen; however, with focus, you can begin to discover when you listen well and when you do not. This provides the starting point for discovering your ideal listening states.

IN PRACTICE

To listen better, we must discover when we are not listening or are half-listening. We must learn how to interrupt our not-listening and half-listening and begin listening. The approach uses body awareness to increase self-awareness in the moment.

Each of us has at least one body each for not-listening, one body for half-listening, and still another body for listening. Listening self-awareness can be developed by cultivating awareness of your three kinds of listening bodies. Once you can discover, in the moment, that you are not listening, you can replace your not-listening body with your listening body, and then, you listen.

1. Discover your not-listening and half-listening bodies:
   a. Sit and think of a conversation in which you felt judgmental about what another person was saying.
   b. Close your eyes.
   c. Recall what the other person said.
   d. Then recall what you said to yourself about what the other person was saying.
   e. Keep imagining the conversation until the experience of the conversation takes over your body.
   f. Notice your posture: slumping, tilting, erect, leaned back, chest out, chest in...
   g. Notice where in your body you are holding tension. This is one of your half-listening bodies.
   h. How do you feel, being in your half-listening body?

2. Discover your listening body.
   a. Sit and think of a conversation which you found engrossing and enthralling.
   b. Close your eyes. Recall what others said.
   c. Recall what you said to yourself about what the other person was saying.
   d. Keep imagining the conversation until the experience

of the conversation takes over your body.

   e. Notice your posture: slumping, tilting erect, leaned back, chest out, chest in…

   f. Notice where in your body you are holding tension. This is one of your half-listening bodies.

   g. How do you feel, being in your half-listening body?

3. During meetings:

   a. Sit in your listening body.

   b. Focus on what is being said, word for word.

   c. Be on the alert for internal voices.

   d. When you find them, quiet them down, go back to your listening body, and focus on what is being said, word for word.

4. Ask teammates, family, and friends:

   a. When do I listen well?

   b. How can they tell that I am listening well?

   c. When do I listen badly?

   d. How can they tell?

5. Experimenting: What happens to your listening when you:

   a. Relax your shoulders and your neck?

   b. Keep your hands in your lap?

   c. Lean forward?

   d. Lean back?

   e. Focus on the voice of the person speaking?

   f. Close your eyes?

   g. Exhale two counts, inhale one count?

   h. How does each of these influence your listening?

SUMMARIZING: LET ME SEE IF I UNDERSTOOD WHAT YOU SAID

John D. Rockefeller once summarized a discussion thus: "I believe that I just heard each of you seven gentlemen express opposition to Standard buying the Lima fields. Please tell me if I misheard." All seven present confirmed that he had heard correctly. The issue was clear. The board's position was clear.

Summarizing is useful. It reduces the cost of miscommunication. It gives the speaker a visceral sense that the summarizer is interested in what the speaker says. It gives everyone else another chance to hear what was said. Teams that summarize improve communication and goodwill within the team. It is very useful when resolving conflict, solving difficult problems, coordinating complex collaboration, and healing ill will.

At one of my long-term clients in the software business, AutoFlow, the engineering group and the business unit had been fighting for seven years. For those seven years, the business unit's general manager tried to influence engineering with anger and intimidation. The resulting antagonism between the two functions cast a pall over all projects within the business unit.

The new general manager asked for my help: "I want to get engineering to listen to me and my team." I said, "You must listen to them before you can expect them to listen to you." The top three executives from engineering and the top three from the business unit met for a day. The day began with tension and superficial friendliness between the two sides. The business unit executives spent the day listening to the engineering executives, summarizing what they heard, and asking questions. They also apologized several times for insults that the engineers had experienced from the business unit's former boss.

This was a challenging day, especially for the business unit executives, who were used to quickly turning conversations into lists of tasks to be completed. By the end of the day, however, humor was exchanged between the two sides.

Then engineering took the initiative to set up a meeting in which they listened to the business unit executives. By the end of the second day, even more humor was exchanged.

Next, I facilitated a weekly project video call, lasting 60 minutes. More than 100 people attended, but only 6 or 7 talked. The tension that existed between the business unit and the engineering executives before their first meeting was also present in the project meeting. I began the meeting by suggesting the rule that one had to summarize what the last person said before sharing one's own point of view. Again, this mode of interaction was challenging and seemed slow initially; however, by the end of the meeting, there was clear agreement to continue using it.

By the end of the first month there was notably less tension. When I talked one-on-one with people, they said that they felt listened to. By the end of the second month, overt friendliness was expressed. When interviewed one-on-one, folks reported feeling respected "by the other side." Near the end of the third month, humor and playfulness broke out; folks acknowledged "really liking their counterparts in the 'other functions.'" Those attending from the support organizations expressed relief and satisfaction.

Summarizing feels strange and awkward at first. Once communication errors are detected and corrected before work is done, motivation starts to build toward wanting to summarize. Besides significantly lowering the cost of rework due to miscommunication, summarizing gives the speaker an explicit experience of being heard. It signals that the listener wants to hear and understand the speaker. In this way, summarizing also builds trust.

In a substantive discussion, it is useful to summarize each paragraph. Summarizing slows down discussion while it speeds up common understanding. I have many favorite stories about the power of summarizing. I will limit myself to adding just one more.

At an R&D lab at Halogen, when I first sat in on a project team meeting, the team was having deep, important technical discussions with toxic bitterness, and "That is the stupidest thing I ever heard" was a typical statement. I interviewed each team member separately after the meeting. No one wanted the meanness. No one knew how to stop it in others or in themselves.

Here also, we invoked the summarizing rule. Summarize first, then share your point of view. Summarizing slowed down the discussion significantly. I had observed that the faster their rhythm, the more hurtful the meanness.

As a result, we established a second rule: Call out anything that seems mean. I modeled calling out meanness. I was the only one to do it for several meetings but then first one, then a second, and quickly after, a third and fourth member summarized and called out meanness without prompting. We audio-recorded the meetings. When individuals were flagged for meanness, they were given the audio to take home and listen to. The rule was, "Listen to yourself being mean. Describe what you do that is mean. Then report back to the team next week." When I was the only one identifying and interrupting, meanness declined slightly. Once others began calling out meanness, it surfaced less and less often. Over the next couple of months, meanness disappeared. Five months later, the team was discussing difficult technical disagreements with humor. I thought, "This will be a halcyon period in each team member's career." Each of the four members of this team I was able to interview five years later said that had been the best experience of their careers, so far.

In these cases, summarizing captures how well the intended, sent message was received by the summarizer. The experience of being heard opens the heart.

- The speaker is offered the opportunity of feeling heard. The speaker can experience the summarizer as committed to hearing the sender.

- The next speaker is forced to consider what they are about to say and make it relevant to what was said.

These two effects are invaluable. They enable participants to acknowledge each others' arguments and reduce the tendency for mean, stinging, or dismissive retorts. In the Halogen R&D example, even this was not enough, but the device of having people call out meanness and having people listen to themselves added another level of accountability and awareness to all involved.

Another less obvious benefit is that the practice of summarizing gives everybody in the room the ability to interrupt a heated situation by asking for a summary. "I'm getting lost, could someone please summarize what Jimmy and Kavitha just said?" When two people are in a heated discussion, it is useful to have each summarize the other. This takes the sting out of a discussion and grounds everybody back to trying to understand what is being said.

Summarizing slows down the discussion rhythm. It gives all participants the opportunity to hear it again.

This has a genuine cost at the beginning of the practice; however, there is good news here. First, taking more time for summaries is easily worth it if what is replaced is fractious, painful exchanges that do not resolve issues. Second, with practice, the group will feel its way into the moments when summarization is and is not useful. Lastly, as the group meets more regularly, the level of comprehension of each person's point of view increases. This makes it easier to understand points and a higher level of trust generally ensues; you are listening to me now.

There are two main ways to introduce summarization into a discussion. The most straightforward is with agreement of the group, or at least the group leader and the identification of a facilitator. This facilitator does not have to be an external person or the leader of the group (in fact, it is often better if they are not the leader).

On one team, someone asked if being the facilitator could make a person into a scapegoat. The facilitator is at risk of being scapegoated if they do a bad job of facilitating—for example, showing bias toward or against an idea or person. I facilitated poorly more than once. In one case, with the leadership team of a nationally renowned nonprofit, at several key moments I failed to ask for a summary. This led me to appear biased against a member of the team, significantly tainting the meeting discussion flow and amplifying difficulties already present. So, there are risks in facilitating poorly and one of the risks is being scapegoated. However, this is not a typical experience; in most cases meeting participants are extremely grateful to the facilitator and recognize that it is difficult to execute the role perfectly.

There will also be times where people will "jump in" with a point they want to make unexpectedly or even try to change the subject. At these times the facilitator also needs to be firm in asking for summaries. Saying things like "Please allow me to summarize what you just said…then…please help me understand how your comment is a response to what Jerry just said," then… "Who wants to summarize Jerry and then respond to what he said?"

It is important to be evenhanded in asking for summaries and not give some in the conversation a pass when others are called upon. Inconsistency can lead to resentment. Instead of asking a specific person to summarize, ask generally, "Would someone please summarize?" The rule should also apply to the leader of the meeting. In fact, it should often especially apply to the leader of the meeting, who is often one of the speakers most likely to wield power, cut across a speaker, or create a subject change.

IN PRACTICE

1. When listening, do not talk to yourself.
2. Listen word for word.
3. Commit yourself to summarizing all substantive utterances for one meeting a day, for a month.
4. Let each meeting know what you are doing.
5. Inquire of participants in each meeting about your summarizing.

      a. When did summarizing work well?

      b. When did it get in the way?

6. Keep a diary. Note the range of responses to your summarizing.

7. When summarizing, maintain a soft and steady gaze at the person you are summarizing. Note any nonverbal response that might indicate you summarized incorrectly: a blink, a slight nod of the head, rolling of the eyes…

      a. Then ask, "Please modify my summary so it suits your intent."

      b. How does it feel to summarize?

8. How to introduce summarization:

      a. Suggest the simple summarization rule for one or two important topic conversations in your team and try this out.

      b. If you do not have control of the meetings but would like to illustrate the utility of this for yourself, consider just applying the protocol to yourself and summarizing a speaker before making your own points.

      c. Observe the room during a discussion and identify who seems to be understanding others and who seems absorbed in their own thoughts before they speak.

INQUIRING: WHAT WOULD HAPPEN IF…?

Just as listening seems like a simple proposition, so does inquiry. What could be simpler than asking a question? Apart from the obvious fact that often important questions are simply never asked, there are many subtleties in question asking which affect the outcome.

A subtle example of questioning gone wrong occurred at AutoFlow. The leadership team was stuck debating a complex set of interconnected strategy choices for the coming year. One of the executives was trying to facilitate the discussion by asking questions.

When it came to a key impasse in the debate, he asked what everybody thought the impact of a key choice would be. This was a useful inquiry, but then he very quickly went on to answer the question himself. This kicked off the discussion of that specific solution, but it did not air what others were thinking or what other ideas there might be.

If he had instead asked, "What do the rest of you think?" the inquiry would have continued. But he did not ask, and the inquiry died there.

Afterwards I said to him: "You posed the question. You posed it well. Then you immediately gave your answer, before anyone had a chance to speak. When you pose a question, always let others answer before you."

By not letting others answer the question, the executive had denied others in the room the chance to answer an important question. The session did ultimately lead to decisions, but they did not feel shared. Be aware, though, that often a decision needs to be made and implemented before a consensus is possible.

The Power of Inquiry

The business unit at AutoFlow mentioned above, was one of four business units competing for the mindshare, and time, of the sales force. The leaders of the unit felt that they were not getting their fair share of sales. The unit's head of marketing decided to find what they could do to get more of sales's mindshare and time. He met with the head of North American sales (NA).

Marketing: You spend less than 10 percent of your time selling our products, is that right?

NA: It is.

Marketing: How come? Why don't you spend more time selling our products?

NA: Selling your products is too much work with little payoff. Of the four business units, your products are the most complex to learn and the most time-consuming to sell. Take the server. It sells itself. Very little time and effort is needed for a great payoff.

Marketing: What makes our products too much work to sell?

NA: You have 14 complex products. To know them well enough to sell them requires more time than I have to invest.

Marketing: Are you saying that if we had one or maybe two offerings that were easy to learn and easy to sell, we would get more of your time and mindshare for selling them?

NA: You got it.

Inquiry has the power to create learning, trust, common understanding, and common purpose. It is needed to look more deeply into an issue or another point of view. Few individuals and teams ask enough questions. In most team conversations, members take their turn to advocate their point of view. Seldom does someone seem curious or interested enough to ask questions.

In many discussions, individuals respond to inquiry defensively. In some cases, the intent of inquiry is to discredit the other person's point of view. These are essential characteristics of defensive teamwork.

Sincere inquiry seeks relevant information and seeks to cultivate deeper understanding. Sincere inquiry builds trust, common understanding, and common purpose. These are the foundation stones for excellent team communication.

Varieties of Inquiry

There are various ways to inquire. We hear an ambiguity and wish to clarify it. We hear an interesting opinion and wish to know the facts behind it. A tool kit of questions that enable one to inquire is useful.

1.   Clarify an ambiguity: *Would you please give us an example?*

2.   Uncover the facts behind the opinion: *What data informs your opinion?*

3.   Discover causal links: *If you said to him what you just said to me, how do you think he would respond?* Then, *What experience leads you to believe that he will think you are being rude? What happens if he thinks you are rude?*

4.   Deepen understanding: *You are strongly advocating option A. Jane is just as strongly advocating option C. I have several questions for you. What do you think happens if we go with option C? And how do you know? What is your data?*

Ideally, inquiring becomes a habit. It becomes a habit with conscious practice. It is useful to cultivate a nose for ambiguity, an eye for causal statements, and an ear for inconsistencies and contradictions.

Just as with summarizing, inquiry should be evenhanded. If someone on the team continually asks a few specific people questions and is much less attentive to others, it can appear that different team members are being held to different standards. In another dynamic, organizations often have decisions or facts that cannot be questioned. This can mean entire conversations happen in the context of missing information or missing motivations.

The only way to address such negative dynamics is to slowly build up the culture of inquiry within the team.

A most efficient way of promoting inquiry in your team is to have an expert facilitator who prompts inquiry in key meetings; yet anyone on a team can take responsibility for inquiring. On teams and in groups in which I am not the expert facilitator, I ask a lot of questions: "Can you say more, please?" "What leads you to believe that?" "What do others think about what was just said?" "What is your experience of what we just read?"

Meetings in which there is mostly just advocacy tend to feel oppressive. It is rare that the next person to speak addresses what was said by those who spoke before, and what they say often crowds out the statements that have gone before. It often feels like people are making speeches, mostly to strangers. Participants tend to half-listen.

Meetings in which there is thoughtful, provocative inquiry tend to feel more alive. Participants recognize each other. Asking someone a question is a way of reaching out, of showing interest. Participants feel connected. It feels like a team. It seems as if participants pay close attention, even when videoconferencing. Participants listen. If participants summarize what is said, those summaries rarely need correction.

Done well, inquiry has a way of changing the dynamics of a conversation that is very powerful. It is also something that can be used by even a few participants to change the whole tenor of a meeting for the positive. Asking questions changes a pure presentation into a dialogue.

Of course, inquiry can also be used maliciously to derail narratives by asking rhetorical or aggressive questions.

The key to the effective use of inquiry is always to ensure the question is 1) directly relevant to what has been said (which means listening is key), and 2) is a genuine request for information from the speaker and not a rhetorical device for seizing the floor to explain a different point of view.

IN PRACTICE

1. Pick three meetings in the coming week in which you will commit yourself to inquire.
    a. Look at the agenda and prereading.
    b. Identify ambiguities that allow you to ask clarifying questions.
    c. Write out your clarifying questions.
    d. Identify causal statements.
    e. Write out your questions to deepen your understanding of each causal statement.

      f. After the meeting, ask participants what questions you asked that added value to the meeting and what questions you asked that did not add value.

      g. Ask participants if it would be valuable for you to ask questions in future meetings.

      h. Keep a diary. After each meeting, note how it felt to inquire. Note the feedback you received from others about your inquiring.

2. At social events, play the following game: Avoid having to talk about yourself by asking questions of whoever you are engaged with.

      a. Ask a question.

      b. Summarize the answer.

      c. Ask your next question.

      d. Summarize the answer.

      e. Continue to repeat a. through d.

3. Practice identifying ambiguity. Listen to recordings of key exchanges.

      a. Identify ambiguities.

      b. For each, write out your clarifying question.

4. Practice identifying causal statements. Listen to recordings of key exchanges.

      a. Identify causal statements.

      b. Write out your "If...then" questions.

5. After meetings, note in your diary how you felt inquiring.

ADVOCATING: OPINIONS NEED FACTS

As we saw in the dialogue between the head of the business unit, marketing, and the head of sales at AutoFlow, the business unit had a very complex set of products. This complexity meant that a lot of functionality was available but also made it hard to articulate the value of the products. The marketing team often grumbled about the complexity of the product set and argued that it should be simplified; however, while there was agreement in principle that this would be a "good thing," the steps needed to do this were complex and never reached a high enough priority.

After a particularly tough set of sales results, the head of marketing got the table's attention at a staff meeting. He said, "I just surveyed the top five people in North American sales. I spoke to each of them for over an hour. I asked them how much of their time they spend selling our products. Each of them said, 'less than 10 percent.' I asked each of them why so little, what would have to change so they would invest more of their time selling our products. Each of them said the same thing, 'There are too many products. They are all complex. There is too much to learn for so little payoff.'"

The head of marketing asked his team, "So, my question is this; Is this a good enough, big enough, data sample to base a change of policy on? These are the five top salespeople in North America, including the head. What do you think? Is this enough data, or do you want more, and if so, from whom?" Everyone around the table thought this was a good enough sample.

The head of marketing continued, "I have been thinking a lot about this, and I have an idea. I can share it now, or I can wait until we have heard from the rest of the table." Encouraged to share his idea, he said, "Sales needs fewer products, simpler to learn and sell. I suggest we figure out how to create two or three bundles that are simple to learn and sell."

Advocating a particular position or idea is the most complex of the communication competencies. It is ubiquitous. Almost every time someone talks, they are advocating. It is how we communicate instructions, directions, problem solutions, options, decisions, performance feedback, policy positions, and on and on.

Advocacy is useful when done well. When advocacy is not done well, however, it is often problematic. There is a set of common errors in advocacy:

- Most advocacy is ambiguous. This means that the statement being advocated can be interpreted, with equal validity, in more than one way.

- Often advocacy is rich in opinion and poor in facts. The absence of facts significantly increases the difficulty of producing productive rational conversation and thought.

- Advocacy is seldom coupled with a request that it be summarized or coupled with inquiry, "What do you think about what I just said?" Competent advocacy incorporates opinion, facts, a request for a summary, and then inquiry.

Practice is necessary to master advocacy, but it is not sufficient. There is an emotional/psychological challenge as well. When we advocate, we experience a desire to exercise influence over others' decisions and solutions. We experience a strong desire to be right. We experience a strong desire to avoid being wrong.

When these psycho-emotional impulses are active, they are accompanied by several behaviors. We try to influence others by controlling what they know. We do this by emphasizing some things, and de-emphasizing others while hiding that we are doing this. When we use these behaviors, we are often unaware of doing so.

Productive Advocacy

A formula for productive advocacy follows: Opinion is coupled with facts, followed by a request to be summarized, and then inquiry. In other words, rather than simply expressing an opinion that something should be different, follow a pattern.

We'll take the head of marketing's argument for product bundles from AutoFlow and enrich it:

- Facts: "I just surveyed the top five people in North American sales. I spoke to each of them for over an hour. I asked them how much of their time they spend selling our products. Each of them said, 'less than 10 percent.' I asked each of them why so little, what would have to change so they would invest more of their time selling our products. Each of them said the same thing, 'There are too many products. They are all complex. There is too much to learn for so little payoff.'"

- Inquiry: "So, my question is this; Is this a good enough, big enough data sample to base a change of policy on? These are the five top salespeople in North America, including the head. What do you think?"

- Opinion: "I have been thinking a lot about this, and I have an idea," and "The salespeople need fewer products, simpler to learn and sell. I suggest we figure out how to create two or three bundles that are simple to learn and sell."

- Summary: "Would somebody please summarize what I just said?"

- Inquiry: "What do you think of what I just said?

Though this approach may seem a little elaborate, it is far more powerful than trying to sway a room with opinion and emotion alone. In particular:

- The presence of facts that others acknowledge creates a foundation that deepens understanding.

- The opinion that is offered is placed in the context of these facts.

- The two inquiries separately ask for agreement on the facts and the opinion.

- The final inquiry invites others present to respond.

It is useful to cultivate several good habits regarding advocacy, facts, and opinions. One is to scan for facts and opinions, noting when facts are missing and when opinions are confused with facts. The second is to always couple facts and opinions when advocating.

Unproductive Advocacy

There are several forms of unproductive advocacy. There is bullying: "Anyone with a brain realizes Option A is the only way to go." Of course, there are leaders who shun anyone who disagrees with them. Lyndon Johnson was a master of bullying. When Frank Church arrived in the Senate from Idaho, his first vote was against Johnson's wishes. Whenever Church approached Johnson after that, Johnson would turn his back on him. He gave Church none of the committee assignments he asked for. He refused to recognize Church's existence.

The chief marketing officer of my data storage company client, Harpers, said, during budget meetings, "We will do $30 million our first year. We have many prospects inside the five-yard line." When the other executives went into the field to meet prospects, they found no prospect within the five-yard line.

When I was a teaching fellow, I said to my class, "Papers are due next week." When several students said the paper was due in two weeks, I did not inquire, instead, I insisted they were due in a week. The students were right. I was wrong. Then I had to face an angry class.

Then there is the leading question, "Option A is the way to go, right?" President Lyndon Johnson feared the conservative response to his withdrawing from Vietnam. He was afraid that he would be seen as the first American president to lose a war. This was a faulty assumption because President James Madison had already lost a war (the War of 1812). America was losing the Vietnam War. The Pentagon insisted that the only way for America to win was to rapidly increase the US force in Vietnam. With the answer a foregone conclusion, President Johnson insisted there was only one option: escalation.

There is also the obfuscation of essential facts. Sometimes obfuscation is good and sometimes necessary. Eight days before the Japanese attack on Pearl Harbor, the permanent undersecretary of the British Foreign Office wrote in his diary, "The Americans withdrew from all substantive discussion with the Japanese and expect to be attacked within two weeks." That was the secret. The attack was not a surprise; it was provoked and expected. Before the attack, a majority of Americans were against direct involvement in the war. After the attack, a huge majority were for direct involvement in the war.

IN PRACTICE

1. Listen to a recording of an interesting exchange during a meeting.
   a. Note the stated opinions and facts.
   b. Note the percentage of opinions that are coupled with facts.
   c. For every opinion lacking facts, write down the questions that will reveal the facts.
2. Think of someone you would like to give feedback to.
   a. Describe what the person currently does.
   b. Describe what you would like the person to do differently.
   c. Describe what changes if the person follows your feedback.
3. Write a two-column case in which you give the feedback.
   a. To prepare, as clearly as you can, articulate each point you want to communicate in the discussion.
   b. To prepare, as clearly as you can, articulate the questions you want to ask.
   c. Now the two-column case: In the left-hand column write what you and others say publicly.
   d. In the right-hand column write what you are thinking and feeling but not saying publicly.
   e. Compare your statements in a. With your statements in c.

f. What information is included in the a. statements that are missing from the c. statements?

g. How do you predict meeting participants would respond if you stated the a. statement rather than the c. statement?

h. How do you know that is how they will respond?

i. All words of judgment should be limited to the right-hand column.

j. The left-hand column should be rich in descriptors.

FACTS VERSUS OPINION: HOW TO SEPARATE THEM

At my software client, Halogen, three product groups had to transition to using the same operating system. There were three operating systems labs. During the integration of three into one, a profound technological disagreement appeared to surface. Many worried that the disagreement might be irreconcilable.

In the midst of a winter storm, the top 35 people from the newly integrated lab met at the O'Hare Hilton in Chicago. We started meeting first thing Monday morning and were scheduled to go eight hours a day through Thursday. On Thursday morning, the agenda finally addressed the profound technological disagreement. It might seem crazy that the most important issue was put off until last. The leader thought that if he put the issue up closer to the front of the retreat and it did not go well, it would undermine anything useful being done during the rest of the retreat. But, by the time we got to Thursday, much good will was evident across all three labs. It was demonstrated by the playfulness observed across lab boundaries.

When we gathered on Thursday morning there was great tension. Each of the former labs presented its operating system. They identified the essential code that they thought had to be retained.

Folks from the other labs asked many questions, both clarifying and substantive. Would you please give me an example of that? What would happen if you did it this way rather than your way? How do you know? What experiments have you completed? How does this actually work?

As the advocacy and inquiry went on, it was clear that each lab had developed its own technical language that prohibited the labs from communicating with each other about technology. The more they separated the nomenclatures from function and code, the more they discovered the agreements were more profound than the disagreements. Finally, we arrived at the core of the disagreement. A half-hour inquiry revealed a difference in nomenclature that hid an agreement about function and code.

With this discovery, the resolution was simple. Morale soared. Collaboration in designing the new operating system excelled. Working through the issues in the snowstorm created the foundations for an essential common language and understanding. Trust and mutual respect rose.

I shared this story with a friend, who responded, "I find it difficult to imagine so much exchange happens after so much holding back." Here is my response: First the group had three days of practicing the communication tools together. By Thursday they had successfully resolved several important issues. Their confidence in the process was growing. Each day they got better at using the tools. Everyone had avoided the technology question for fear that discussion would make things worse. My participation gave them some confidence that something useful could result from a discussion. Everyone was eager to share their systems. Based on the few corrections needed on summaries, people listened very well. In the end, what really helped was that there was no technology disagreement. The differences were in language. No one was nearly so attached to their language as they were to their technology.

This story illustrates two levels of disconnection between participants. The first is the terminology disconnect that, until carefully examined, made it appear that there were fundamental disagreements. The second was the anxiety, defensiveness, and concern among all the parties about this perceived conflict: Who would prevail? Would a poor solution be chosen? What if this issue could not be resolved? These perceptions and doubts had persisted so long that an intensive meeting in a snowstorm was needed.

The root of the resolution required productive advocacy that coupled facts and opinions plus lots of summarizing, and lots of inquiry. All participants reported feeling that they had been well listened to by participants from the other labs. Morale and trust improved dramatically.

One very useful strategy to help separate fact from opinion is making a conscious distinction between describable and indescribable things.

What Can Be Described

1. Actions

    a. A decision: *Marilyn cut the budget for food by 20 percent and the budget for photocopying by 50 percent.*

    b. Decision process: *When deciding what to do about the food budget, she sought input from no one on the program staff. She consulted only finance.*

    c. The implementation of a decision or plan: *She let the program staff know by email three days before the retreat was scheduled to start.*

    d. The impact of the action or behavior: *This took the whole retreat staff by surprise and created a frenzy of busywork. Staff members said that they felt undermined and uncared for. Instead of the usual pre-retreat excitement and group discussion after dinner, everyone went to their rooms and spent the evening alone.*

2. Behaviors

    a. What was said, word for word: *He said, "No, I didn't like or approve of your leadership."*

    b. Voice - volume, tone, pitch, speed, rhythm: *He said this in a much lower register than he usually speaks. He literally dropped from tenor to basso. He talked faster.*

    c. Facial expressions—movements of the forehead, eyebrow, eyelids, cheeks, lips, jaw, skin tone: *You know how he usually smiles when he talks. This time he squinted, his mouth was turned down, his lips pursed.*

    d. Posture of the head and trunk: *His trunk leaned forward, chest out. He bobbed his head forward and back.*

    e. Gestures of the head, trunk, arms, and hands: *He kept pointing his right first finger at my face, his right elbow firmly planted on the table. He pointed his first right finger straight at my eye.*

3. Facts

    a. Measurements

    b. Percentages /Ratios

    c. Dates

    d. Budgets

    e. Balance sheets

What Cannot Be Accurately Described

1. Others' intentions and motivations: *He was critical of the evening because we did not ask him to teach last year.*

2. The emotions of others: *He was angry and hurt.*

3. What others think: *He thought he was a better teacher than the senior rabbi.*

A refined awareness of facts and opinions—of when opinions lack facts, and of when opinions are confused with facts—is very useful. It makes planning, implementing, and problem solving easier. Helping teammates refine their awareness improves teamwork.

IN PRACTICE

1. Think of an unresolved work problem.
   a. State the facts of the problem.
   b. List some of the opinions that participants have articulated.
   c. Which opinions are backed by facts?
   d. What are the facts of each opinion?
   e. What opinions are not backed by facts?
   f. What questions do you ask to reveal the facts?

2. Think of an upcoming difficult conversation.
   a. List the competing and/or conflicting opinions regarding the issue.
   b. State the facts regarding the difficult issue that needs to be discussed.
   c. Which opinions are backed by facts?
   d. What are the facts of each opinion?
   e. What opinions are not backed by facts?
   f. What questions would you ask to reveal the facts?

3. Think of difficult feedback you have to give to someone or to a team.
   a. Describe what is currently being done.
   b. Describe the consequences of what is being done.
   c. Describe the changes that should be made in what is being done.
   d. Predict the value these changes will bring about.

4. When disagreements threaten to derail a discussion:
   a. As the parties describe their approach again from first principles, highlight the assumptions they are making and how their solutions follow from the assumptions and reasoning.
   b. Ensure that everyone in the room has the same understanding of the terms being used by each side.

c. For each of the "facts" being stated as obvious by a party, ask them (and then the group) to determine whether this is really a fact, an opinion, or an assumption with some degree of certainty.

INTERRUPTING INTERRUPTIONS: EXCUSE ME, YOU INTERRUPTED SAM...

Interruptions are insidious. Often unnoticed, they can quickly become established in a communications culture. More dominant and assertive speakers interrupt more. Their interruptions are accepted. Less assertive speakers accept being interrupted

Interruptions leave people feeling unheard. Ideas and observations are left unvoiced. A discussion with many interruptions can also feel very productive with new ideas flowing freely. However, even in the cases where it feels good to have ideas appearing every minute, interruptions can be harmful in that these good ideas can get lost as they are bulldozed out of the discourse by the next round of interruptions.

A good meeting moderator can help by giving the floor to each participant in an organized manner, but even this is limited in its effect. This technique assumes everybody has equal confidence speaking on every topic or that the moderator knows who wishes to speak up when. Those given the floor still often get pushed aside by excitable interrupters.

So how can we slow down interruptions and reduce the number of missed points, and lower the frustration levels for more timid speakers?

I led a study group consisting of 10 senior independent management consultants in Silicon Valley for four years. Two years after the group started, a new member, Jeff, joined. Jeff was very successful at designing and leading training programs. He was also a brilliant diagnostician of complex organizational issues. However, he estimated that he had been fired from at least half of the organizational development projects he led.

In the first two hours of the first meeting of the study group that Jeff attended, he interrupted others four times. I interrupted his second two interruptions. After my second interruption, Jeff asked the group, "Did I really interrupt four times?" Members of the group assured him that he had. Jeff expressed surprise. He was unaware of interrupting. Over the next five hours, Jeff interrupted another six or seven times. Just before the meeting ended, Alice, another member, asked Jeff, "Is this how you behave when you are consulting?" Jeff said he did not know, but he imagined so. Alice suggested that he bring two audiotapes to our next meeting, one, she suggested, of his consulting and one of his training.

After listening to the two tapes at the next meeting, George said to Jeff, "In the training tape, you listened and inquired. In the consulting tape, you interrupted and advocated. If I had a consultant who interrupted constantly, I would fire him, too."

Jeff asked the group's help in learning to avoid interrupting. He asked us to interrupt his interruptions. We did. By Jeff's sixth meeting he did not interrupt once.

The biggest secret to reducing interruptions is making them visible and highlighting when they happen. This creates two opportunities: first, the interrupters realize they need to hold their thoughts and perhaps act differently next time; second, it creates the opportunity for the interrupted speaker to continue and articulate what they wanted to say. Both of these are important.

Calling out interruptions like this when ideas are free-flowing can sometimes feel disruptive to a creative process, but it is possible to mitigate these disruptions. If interruptions keep happening (and even interruptions of interruptions), designate someone to begin noting down the points everyone is making, then give air time to each person in turn. This approach creates a list of useful points to explore when the conversation slows down a little.

When I began attending quarterly offsite meetings with the AutoFlow leadership team, the interruptions were constant. Each interruption changed the subject of discussion. Not only were there interruptions; several conversations were going on at the same time. It was a madhouse. I began interrupting the interruptions. When two conversations were going on simultaneously, I would shout, "One conversation at a time, please!"

Midway through the second quarterly offsite, I no longer had to shout, "One conversation at a time, please." By the end of the third offsite, there were no interruptions to be interrupted. To change this team's two bad habits required my forceful, but friendly, consistent facilitation. Every member of the team hailed the improvements.

A final point here is that anyone in the room can say the words "Excuse me, but you just interrupted Sam." This doesn't need to be the meeting moderator (who might even be the interrupter). It requires courage, at first, to interrupt an interruption. Eventually, it will seem natural.

IN PRACTICE

1. Invite your team to experiment with interrupting interruptions.
2. Agree to the duration of the experiment. A month is suggested as a reasonable time of experimentation.
3. Come to a preliminary agreement on:
   a. When is it appropriate to interrupt an interruption?
   b. What should be said when interrupting an interruption?
4. Think about each ongoing meeting.
   a. In each meeting, who interrupts whom?

  b. What does the interrupter do to interrupt?

5. Think about how you will interrupt each interruption.

  a. What sounds, gestures, and movements will you make to get the meeting's attention?

  b. What will you say, once you have the meeting's attention?

  c. Practice a. and b. until they become second nature.

PART III

Communications Culture and Essential Processes

A good meeting doesn't just achieve its purpose; it also strengthens the bonds between the participants. Such meetings show them that they can collaborate, that they can craft shared goals, and that the others in the room can understand their points of view.

When I first met many of the teams I have worked with, I found that they took their communication patterns as fixed and static. They assumed that communications were as good as they were going to get and focused on navigating the existing patterns, taboos, and idiosyncrasies of the group.

Reflection on one's own individual behavior, on the behavior of each team member, and on the team itself is the path to making a real difference in communication. This is the beginning of hard but extremely gratifying work.

Thirty years after I first worked with an architectural firm mentioned in Part II, the founders sold the firm to three partners. I began team-building with the three partners a year before they were to take control.

A month after the new partners took control, I interviewed the firm's ten associates.

Under the founders, who were husband and wife, the structure had been very flat. The wife managed the staff and operations, and the husband took the lead on strategy and marketing. The wife was a really smart, highly intuitive, angelic autocrat who never put her or her partner's interests above anybody in the firm.

I interviewed the 10 associates over the course of a week using hour-long, one-on-one confidential interviews. I was deeply impressed with the high emotional intelligence of all but one associate. I was also impressed with how the associates thought about managing projects and architects. Under the current structure over 70 architects and 50 or more projects were managed by two people. All of the associates wanted better communication and collaboration. I thought a better structure was to delegate authority for supervising jobs and architects to the associates.

The partners were reluctant to change anything, at first. The partners and I had six hours of intense, challenging, productive conversations over my proposal that the associates manage the staff. They agreed to implement it. Over the course of a month, in weekly hour-and-a-half meetings, the three partners, with my facilitation, decided what responsibilities and authority they would delegate to the associates.

Two months after the reorganization was implemented, one of the partners said to me, "The old firm espoused democracy, but it was a gentle, caring autocracy. Now we have true democracy."

This evolution of the firm involved not only communications breakthroughs but also changes in responsibility, ways of doing things, and the growth of trust amongst partners and among partners and associates.

The most important lesson was that while listening, summarizing, being curious about what others think, and asking questions are all important in individual meetings, it is the change in culture over time that delivers the dramatic transformation of the team. A single good meeting adds a valuable brick to a foundation and opens up possibilities that were not there before, but it is the regular repetition of these successes and the continuation of positive communication between meetings that delivers the real long-term benefit.

This section covers some of the structural aspects that need to be taken care of so that good communication over the long term can flourish.

- Section 1: Making communication a priority
- Section 2: Inclusive decision making
- Section 3: Setting agendas
- Section 4: Discussion focus: do we go deep or wide?
- Section 5: Scoring and champions: techniques for ranking
- Section 6: Communication between meetings
- Section 7: Is it time to stop talking?

PRIORITIES: MAKING COMMUNICATION A PRIORITY

Modern work schedules are busy, often with many interactions and interruptions throughout the day. Standing meetings, special topics, quick calls, one-on-ones. All these claims on time seriously affect the ability to do "actual work." Or do they?

Certainly, there is a tendency to overload on meetings; but in many cases, meetings are the actual work. Decisions often require discussion. When ideas are sought, dialogue can help surface good ones; when functions need to coordinate, when team members are concerned about something, discussion helps.

How can we tell what is good, valuable communication and what is a time sink?

Sam, the general manager of the AutoFlow business unit I worked with, traveled extensively for his role. He met often with customers and stakeholders in the business around the world. He also ran a complex team that required high levels of collaboration. Many meetings were one-offs and dominated the executive's schedule. When it came to his team, there was no regular cadence for staff meetings or one-on-ones.

The leader was responsive to the needs of his team but it was often hard to find a calendar slot, causing pain for him and those wanting to meet. The staff meeting was also canceled on a semi-regular basis due to travel needs. Though this team was happy with the executive they worked for, decision-making within the team often dragged on, and small, yet essential, items never made it onto agendas for discussion. The low-level stress of needing to scramble for meeting times was a drag on the team members.

With prompting, the executive made new commitments to regular meetings: a quarterly three day offsite to air important topics, a more regular cadence to the staff meeting, a shift from a watercooler style to one where people could add key topics to a list before the meeting. As a result, more key topics were surfaced and discussed, and fewer one-off emergency meetings had to be called.

Another benefit was that fewer ad hoc meetings were needed because the whole team knew they could likely get key topics aired at the next staff meeting. Calendar congestion actually dropped when the regular staff meeting was less prone to cancellation.

The lesson here is that having a few "sacred" spots in the calendar for key communication is a very powerful way to structure communication and strengthen the team's culture. People know when the meetings will occur, they can save up topics without having to wonder when a topic can be raised. Adding quarterly team discussions and standing one-on-ones have similar beneficial effects on communication hygiene.

The "sacred" meetings on a calendar will depend on the team itself, but they can be thought of in three broad categories:

- **Regular synchronization (sync) meetings**: these

are at least weekly but may be daily, depending on the responsibility of the team. They focus on the now and on current issues which have arisen for each team member. They should generally avoid deep strategic discussions unless they are preplanned (straying into this territory often means spending a lot of time and still not reaching a conclusion). If the meeting cadence is weekly or longer it can be very helpful to have a working document to which people can add topics for discussion.

- **Planning and deep-dive meetings**: these take a specific topic (staffing, technology roadmap, competitors etc.) which require preparation and take as much time as is needed to tackle it. This may also include monthly, quarterly, or annual planning. They are not the place for day-to-day small issues. Often these types of meetings can be scheduled in an ad hoc way as topics arise. However, it is valuable to acknowledge that a team needs time for these discussions. Having a regular or semi-regular slot in the calendar helps ensure there is space to have these important discussions. On each cycle the most important items can then use these free slots without disrupting everybody's calendar.

- **Team retreats/offsites**: it is highly valuable to have, quarterly or at least twice a year, a slot of a few days in which the team can disconnect from day-to-day issues and consider the big picture. Topics may include some of the planning/deep-dive topics but should also include very long-term views and meta-issues such as communication, how planning is done, etc. Such "retreats" or offsites can take many forms. However, their essential characteristics are that they step back from the day-to-day and tackle both the very long term as a framing for current work and as analysis of the team itself—how its functioning can be improved. In most cases it really helps if this type of meeting (more than all others) can be done in person. However, it is possible to achieve some of the same outcomes virtually. We discuss this in Part V of the book..

Though the regularity of each of these meeting types will vary by team, they are all useful. When deep strategy topics can be pushed to a deep discussion meeting and day-to-day issues are dealt with at a quick cadence, deeper discussions do not become dumping grounds for large numbers of small issues.

In managing the meeting plan, it is important to regularly review the pattern to see if things are working: What is working well enough? What needs to work better? Who might do what differently? Who needs to coordinate better with whom? Where does communication need to improve? What issues need to be addressed next? What in our strategy, policies, and operations needs to be reviewed? Are we finding time to do it?

IN PRACTICE

1. List the meetings you attend per week and month.
2. Total the number of hours you spend per week and month in meetings.
3. Prioritize the meetings according to their importance to your team.
4. At which meetings could you delegate someone to take your place?
5. Which meetings could you drop altogether?
6. For each of the meetings you will continue to attend, what changes might improve the value of the meeting?
   a. How can the process be improved?
   b. What percentage of statements are summarized?
   c. What percentage of stated opinions are accompanied by the relevant facts?

    d. How much inquiry occurs, and of what kind?

    e. How many interruptions are there?

    f. How can the focus be improved?

    g. What changes in attendance would add value to the meeting?

    h. What risks accompany your proposed changes in attendance?

7. Is there a new meeting that would add significant value or save you and your teammates time?

INCLUSIVE DECISION MAKING: THE "WHY AND HOW"

Inclusive decision making requires that all those affected by the decision be given an appropriate opportunity to influence it. The opportunity to influence a decision is not a vote; it is an opportunity to influence.

Here comes a bit of a conundrum that can be managed by inclusive decision making. I have observed, time and again, that strong motivation comes from a strong internal commitment. My mentor, Chris Argyris, said that in modern organizations (except the military), internal commitment can be cultivated by granting participants free, informed choice and valid information. I wondered, "What does this look like?"

A. A. Berle said that individuals, not groups, must make decisions. Consensus decision making creates a power vacuum and is slow. Every one of my client organizations that used consensus decision making was frustrated by its slowness. Worse: the fear of a "vote-based" decision often makes leaders back away from giving others any influence at all, because they feel poor outcomes will result (and they are probably right in many cases).

So, how can we create free and informed choice while giving one individual the power to decide? We cannot, but here is a solution that I have found works well. It is inclusive decision making. One person decides. Everyone else gets to influence the decision and the decision maker.

This may sound a little disingenuous, but it works. The decision maker seeks input from those affected by the decision and from those involved in implementing the decision. In a team setting, or one-on-one, the decision maker hears input from all involved. The decision maker summarizes the input of each participant and then asks clarifying and substantive questions. There may be multiple iterations of this exchange, reflecting the complexity and importance of the decision. Once the decision maker decides, before implementation, the decision maker meets the team, announces the decision, and then explains the reason for the choice of this option rather than others. In the explanation, the decision maker addresses each input that was not accounted for in the decision.

Every team I have worked with which implemented inclusive decision making was satisfied with the improvements in collaboration, communication, and morale. This may seem counterintuitive: Why would people be satisfied with just talking to the decision maker when that person could simply ignore their input? The reality is that their ability to articulate their view is the important thing. If a decision maker subsequently makes rational, fair decisions, then most participants will recognize this. If a decision maker does not explain the decision, then they will likely lose the loyalty of the participants no matter how much communication there is.

Who should attend meetings?

Individuals and representatives of teams, who are responsible for implementing decisions made in the meeting should attend, and individuals and representatives of teams, who have knowledge that is essential to making a well-informed decision should attend.

Inclusive decision making

The executive director of a nonprofit, who I had been working with for a year, told me that she had just discovered that the agency had a budget shortfall and would have to reduce salaries temporarily. She asked me how she might handle this. The staff included nine senior staff with advanced degrees, who led seminars and longer training programs, seven support staff, and the executive director. She followed my suggestion that she call a half-day meeting, attended by all staff. She told them about the shortfall. She said she wanted to hear each staff member's thoughts on how to manage it. The executive director listened, summarized each person's views, and then asked questions. By the end of the meeting, they had a solution. The executive director would take a 30 percent drop in salary, the senior staff would each take a 20 percent drop in salary, and the support staff a 10 percent drop in salary. A month later, I checked in with each staff member, one-on-one, Everyone was happy with the solution. While no one was happy to have their salary level reduced, they understood the need and thought the process fair, inclusive, and efficient.

Inclusive decision making seems to require good listening, good summarizing, and good inquiry. The listening and summarizing give the participant who speaks an explicit, visceral, strong sense of being heard and included. Given the constraints of the decision situation, everyone implementing and affected has the chance to give appropriate input. Inclusiveness deepens individuals' internal commitment to collective action.

Being inclusive means taking a careful approach to considering who should be invited to a meeting, then, at the meeting itself, making sure that everyone's voice is heard. Many of the techniques in previous sections of this book can be applied to enabling all participants to have a voice, but it is useful to be proactive in applying them to pull in each stakeholder on a given topic.

Ways to be inclusive during meetings

When doing a round table, be explicit about the amount of time each person gets to talk. Interrupt people who talk beyond their allotted time. When the discussion is free form, notice who is not participating. Ask nonparticipants what they think. When participants allow themselves to be interrupted, interrupt the interruption, saying something like, "Excuse me, but Sam was not done talking." When you know a participant has a different point of view that is not being expressed, ask them to articulate their point of view.

One of the companies I worked for was Alliance Computer. The organizational division I worked with was The Server Group (TSG). TSG had four primary teams: hardware, operating systems, software, and marketing. Jim was the general manager, Mike was head of hardware, Jay was head of the operating system, Smith was head of software, and Allen was head of marketing. Jim was making decisions about their product on his own without consulting his direct reports. Morale was low. Jim's direct reports felt resentful of Jim's decision-making style. But no one said anything to Jim.

TSG was months behind schedule in getting their product out the door. Allen complained that his teammates were ignoring what he had learned that customers wanted. He worried, also, that without his input, the product would not be competitive.

Jim, puzzled by the poor morale and poor coordination, asked for my help. Once I interviewed his direct reports and their direct reports, the problem with Jim's decision-making style became clear. Jim was making decisions unilaterally without seeking input from those responsible for implementing the decision or those affected by it.

After receiving my findings, Jim met with his team. It was suggested that the team experiment with inclusive decision making. All agreed to give it a try: for every decision, there is one decision maker, and every decision maker would seek input from everyone involved in implementing the decision and everyone affected by the decision. Once the decision maker makes a decision, and when the decision is announced, the decision maker addresses each input that was not accounted for in the decision, explaining why it was not accounted for.

The team met weekly. At first, Jim would forget and make a decision by himself. At the weekly meeting, someone would point this out. Jim would apologize, a little upset with himself. At these moments, members of the team would tell Jim how much his effort was appreciated. Then Jim would rescind the decision, if it had not already been implemented, and would open the decision to the group's input. He would summarize each person's input and then would make the decision. Within two months of the first meeting, Jim had stopped making unilateral decisions. Decision making and implementation improved, taking less time and less effort, with more successful results.

This was a challenging process for everyone involved, but for Jim especially. The team decided to keep using inclusive decision making. They got their product to market on time, and it proved to be more successful than anticipated.

Another client, Lee, who supported his lab with significant Defense Advanced Research Projects Agency (DARPA) contracts, was in his office packing for a trip when I walked in. I asked him where he was going. He said he was going to visit his friends at DARPA. I said, "But they have no money." He stopped his packing, turned, looked me in the eye, and said, "The most important time to visit your friends is when they have no money." Inclusion is essential to communication that builds and sustains morale to the point where it is a strategic advantage. It is important to make sure each member of the team has an appropriate voice in each discussion.

In Practice

1. Who should attend a meeting:
   a. Individuals and representatives of teams who are affected by decisions made in the meeting.
   b. Individuals and representatives of teams who are responsible for implementing decisions made in the meeting.
   c. Individuals and representatives of teams who have knowledge that is essential to making a well-informed decision.
2. Being inclusive during meetings:
   a. When doing a round table, be explicit about the amount of time each person gets to talk.
   b. Interrupt people who talk beyond the allotted time.
   c. When the discussion is free form, notice who is not participating.
   d. Ask nonparticipants what they think.
   e. When participants allow themselves to be interrupted, interrupt the interruption, saying something like, "Excuse, but Sam was not done talking."
   f. When you know a participant has a different point of view that is not being expressed, ask them to articulate their point of view.
3. When making decisions:
   a. Allow everyone affected by the decision to give appropriate input into the decision. No one gets a vote; all affected get a voice.
   b. Once the decision is made, the decision maker meets with those who gave input. The decision maker addresses each input that was not accounted for in the decision and why it was not accounted for.
4. On teams and in communities:
   a. Welcome new members.
   b. Stay in touch when nothing is happening.
   c. Keep others up to date.
   d. Be solicitous of other members of the team.

USING AGENDAS EFFECTIVELY: STRUCTURING DIFFERENT TYPES OF MEETINGS

A common error when planning agendas is to underestimate the time that each topic requires to achieve the discussion's objective. There are two normal responses to this error. One is to rush through agenda items, decreasing the likelihood of satisfying the objectives of each discussion. The other is to not discuss certain agenda items.

When it comes to meeting agendas themselves, setting them well and then sticking to them plays a big role in whether attendees find value in a meeting. The AutoFlow business unit I worked with had significant difficulty in getting the rest of the company to recognize the importance of its set of products. At the corporate level, the team's inputs and content were often given little attention.

The regular monthly briefing call run by Dave, the manager for this team, always started with a look at current results and hot topics. It was attended by both the marketing and product managers as well as sales representatives, about 50 people in all. While Dave always kicked off the meetings in the right way and some meetings went very well, in others a negative result or pushback on a process that had occurred would lead to a long off-agenda discussion. These diversions often took one of the following forms:

- A debate on whether underlying cyclical or other trends might be affecting results, though these were not visible from the data available. These discussions invariably ended with a general acknowledgment of the need for more data, that the data was hard to obtain, and often no action to do so.

- A discussion on the need for new types of content (marketing materials, tutorials, etc.) and what form they should take to serve all regions. These discussions invariably ended with an agreement that such content would be helpful but no clear idea of its priority versus other things.

- A discussion of corporate programs above the level of the business unit and what impact they might have or of why decisions relating to those programs had been taken.

It is not the case that there was no useful information presented in these discussions. They contained insight and, at the very least, were a signal that certain issues were important. However, the team struggled to stay on topic, and they struggled to get through the agenda, and thus, actionable items were left undiscussed. Worse, in most cases, these larger issues recurred often, and they were unresolvable in the meeting.

The desire to address frustrating topics is strong and can derail meetings. When this pattern becomes established, there is not enough time to adequately discuss all the issues that need to be addressed.

A more effective way to deal with this problem is to separate meetings into two types: strategy meetings and operations meetings.

1. **Strategy meetings** deal with things affecting timeframes of the year (possibly multi-year), quarter, or month. They attempt to address hard problems and come up with long-term solutions. They often result in changes to the team plan.

2. **Operations meetings** deal with day-to-day or week-to-week issues in executing the plan. These meetings deal with short-term results, opportunities, and problems. A useful set of inquiry includes, "Who expects to get what from whom, by when, to what quality, and performance specs?" These questions may result in adjustments to the plan but typically steer away from big-picture issues.

The key is to have both types of meetings in the calendar and to recognize which topics belong where. When topics such as systemic failures in the processes for tracking across the marketing funnel arise in an operations meeting, these can be curtailed and added to the agenda for the next strategy meeting. Likewise, for a strategy meeting, day-to-day issues are ideally checked at the door.

A second very useful distinction is between standing and single-issue meetings:

1. **Standing Hot Topics meetings such as regular staff meetings or one-on-ones**: Here there is a predefined scope and attendee list, and the meeting is held regularly. Topics fit within the general scope but focus on what's important in each category at that moment in time.

2. **Single-issue meetings**: These are generally scheduled for the purpose of resolving or advancing a particular topic. These could be short or several days long, the purpose being to resolve a single big issue.

For standing meetings, it is valuable to determine a short set of headings that define the scope of the discussion and prompt attendees to be ready to raise the hot topics they have in these categories. Opening an agenda document ahead of time where attendees can list key topics that they would like covered can be very helpful in time management.

For single-issue meetings it is important that everyone be clear on the objective of the discussion: Learn more about something? Decide on something? In addition, it should be specified what background information participants should review before the meeting and who will play what role in the meeting.

Clearly multiple issues sometimes need to be addressed and the same set of meetings is used to resolve them. Having too many meetings often leads us to make meetings as short as possible. When we shorten meetings, topics suffer from inadequate discussion. This is often a false economy: discussions are not finished, and hence, yet another meeting is needed, the undecided item affects other decisions and the time spent discussing them, and so on.

In the case of Dave's monthly briefing call, the action to take was for Dave to try to shorten the off-topic discussions by capturing the issue in a summary and tasking one of his team to investigate it with the people concerned. This was not always easy, but it allowed those concerned with an issue to be heard (and receive a more considered answer in a future call), and it helped the call to move on closer to its planned agenda.

A final important reason for having enough space in the agenda is to leave time for humanity. Although not every interaction needs it, any meeting for a team which is less regular than weekly benefits hugely from some time for social interactions. For example, a segment at the beginning where people catch up about their weekends, kids' schools, etc. This may feel like wasted time, but it is absolutely key in helping team members grow closer and understand one another better.

Establishing the right meeting patterns for an organization is an art; however, it has a huge payoff: regular standing meetings form the heartbeat of team communication, single-topic meetings feel satisfying when they get to the heart of a matter, and finally resolve into new understanding or decisions.

IN PRACTICE

1. Audit your current standing operational meetings:
   a. What content is relevant to operations?
   b. What content is not relevant to operations?
   c. What should be done with the irrelevant content?
   d. Do strategy issues get discussed?
   e. What impact does this have on the discussion of relevant operating issues?
   f. How often do you run out of time and have to reconvene?
2. On strategy:
   a. What strategic issues and questions cause you concern?

> b. What needs to happen to ease your concern?
> 3. On the meeting's humaneness:
>   a. How does it feel, being in this meeting?
>   b. How would you like it to feel different?
>   c. What can be done to make the desired change?

DISCUSSION FOCUS: DO WE GO DEEP OR WIDE?

In one IT product organization I worked with, the team organized regular quarterly offsites to step out of the day-to-day and review strategy. The team members were engaged and passionate in addressing the issues on the agenda, but it was often very difficult to complete agenda items. The big topics would spill over to the next session and cause other things to be missed. There was a tendency in the team to "deep dive" on individual subproblems or solutions and then not have time to consider other parts of the problem.

Jack: *Ok, let's go round the table and see what options we have to address this.*

Bill: *Well, the first problem is that the delivery team really isn't aligned with our goals and so anything we do is going to be hampered by that.*

Jenny: *I had two meetings with them last week, and they seem to be coming around to our way of thinking. We also talked about their new project that delivers a different online experience that could do some good in the long term too.*

Bill: *We've seen a lot of talk like that before and it normally doesn't get us anywhere.*

Stefan: *What we really need is a better liaison structure—someone on point who has regular check-ins with them, sharing of roadmaps, and so on.*

Jenny: *We have someone who is now doing this.*

This exchange isn't wrong per se, and indeed it can be productive for solving problems; however, the deep dive is likely to last several minutes at least and the original goal of the conversation—to answer the question, "What are our options?"— isn't being addressed. It's possible the problem with the delivery team's goals must be solved for all options, but perhaps not. It may be that there are more promising avenues which do not involve the delivery team at all.

One of the techniques the group introduced to deal with this was to step back and ask the question: Is this a breadth-first or a depth-first discussion? Aptly for an IT team the meaning comes from simple ways of implementing search on computer systems:

- Breadth-first: Looks at all the possible solutions briefly and lists them out next to each other. While this does not tell you much about each solution, it lays out the "breadth of options".

- Depth-First: Takes one of the possible solutions (the first or what seems to be the best) and digs deeper into it by fleshing out further steps. This method evaluates whether a particular solution is valid and how it would work but does not put it into context of other possible solutions.

Both these approaches are valid at different times. What is important is to know what type of conversation needs to be had. Deep diving into the first promising possible solution in significant detail can be a huge waste of time if there are many other options which might also be realistic candidates. On the other hand, if the likely course of action looks clear to everybody at the outset, there is no need to list 10 other solutions.

In these situations, it is useful for the meeting facilitator to be explicit about the conversation to be had:

- If the group is brainstorming possible solutions, focus on breadth first: go around the room gathering options and limiting the discussion of each to a few minutes. Ensure that everyone has a voice and that all the "options" are captured. Prevent deep dives when gathering options.

- Once one or two candidates are clear, assess if the room is ready to anoint one or two as preferred paths to explore. These can then receive a defined amount of meeting time for a more in-depth first discussion. If there are multiple viable solutions, set a time limit for the discussion on each one.

If part of the dynamic in the room is the attachment of some participants to particular solutions, then it can be hard to give other options a fair run at discussion. One way I saw this dealt with was at a startup I worked with, where we applied the following process:

- Step 1: Go through several circuits of the table in which each participant could name and give a one-line description of a solution to discuss. Add these to a whiteboard or flipchart list.

- Step 2: Go round again, asking each participant in turn to pick the next solution to discuss.

- Step 3: Discuss the selected solution for a time-bounded window.

This decouples the idea brainstorming phase of the discussion from topic selection. It also makes sure the breadth of options is visible for all. If the group is too large to have everyone select the topic they would like to cover in turn, Step 2 could be done by going round the room and having each participant flag two or three of the solutions they'd most like to see discussed.

IN PRACTICE

1. Which meetings that you attend need an overview of all available options?
    a. What should be done in preparation?
    b. What questions and issues should be considered in preparation?
    c. Do a roundtable identifying options until the discussion becomes repetitive.
    d. For each breadth meeting, what topics derail the breadth discussion and go unproductively deep?
    e. What should be done about this?
2. Which meetings are depth meetings, requiring deep discussion of one or two options?
    a. What should be read in preparation?
    b. What questions and issues should be considered in preparation?
    c. Do a roundtable until the discussion becomes repetitive.
    d. For each depth discussion, what topics derail the discussion and go unproductively broad?
    e. What should be done about this?

SCORING AND CHAMPIONS: TECHNIQUES FOR RANKING

Sometimes teams are faced with problems that they have no experience with or no precedent to rely on. Sometimes the criteria for the decision fail to distinguish adequately between the available options. Discussing such issues can take a lot of time, make one's head hurt, and be emotionally exhausting. In these cases, more structured discussion methods may be useful. Two different structures are described in this section: Scoring and Champions.

In an IT product organization example, one such case was an upcoming series of decisions on prioritizing projects for a major shift in direction. All parties to the discussion knew that the outcomes would be likely to have some effect on increasing or decreasing focus on the projects in question. These shifts meant, potentially, personal losses or gains in headcount and resources, but, more importantly, the likelihood of large shifts in direction for team members they cared about.

Jack: *We'll need at least two hours to go over priorities, but I can see it lasting much longer.*

Jenny: *Right, how can we cut to the chase and not be too abstract? We've been tiptoeing around these issues, but we just need to start doing things.*

While everyone in the room was collaborative and on board with the new direction, there was significant risk of spending much time in discussion that did not move the team productively toward a decision. The task of the first meeting was to get a clear sense of the status of every project and how it related to the new direction. In each case the project managers responsible provided the overview. How to frame the conversation so it would be productive?

They used a scoring method. The manager for each product gave a score for the project on two dimensions: 1) scoring 0–5 on value to the new business direction, 2) scoring 0–5 on value to the existing business. Then, having given the scores, each elaborated on their reasons for them. This method meant that each project discussion started with a clear statement on potential value up front and words to support that value.

Although the scores themselves ended up being adjusted and not used in a ranking fashion, updates were short and concise with a clear conclusion, helping everyone to get a quick broad picture of status.

Jenny: *Ok, next up is the Synchro product, I don't really know how* *to score this out of 5, but I guess I'll put it at a 3 for relevance to revenue and a 2 for relevance to the new direction. Revenue because it's $100 million per year which is around the same as the Babel project and low relevance because it will probably need a whole different feature set in the new world. It's not clear we have the capacity to do that."*

Jack: *Revenue makes sense, but thinking about relevance: aren't some of the features really important?*

Jenny: *Yes, but for scoring I guess the way I was thinking about that is: keep this at two and create a new entry which is just the A, B, and C features delivered in a stand-alone way on the platform. That offshoot I'd say is priority 5.*

This method can be applied with any type of score relevant to a list that must be prioritized. Again, the scores themselves are not that important, but stating scores upfront forces a clear statement of belief rather than an artfully constructed argument left open to interpretation by everyone else.

This may seem a trivial change—why not skip scores? Surely it is the reasoning that is important? Indeed, the reasoning is what ends up being important. However, unfortunately, without a score, it is very complex to understand how a speaker values a project, and it is also very hard to have a discourse about relative value. When talking about a project close to them, a manager will naturally paint it in a good light even if they recognize it might not be crucial to a new direction. It feels good to say nice things about one team or another. When forced to give scores up front, speakers must give a relative value judgement right up front.

The process of cuts and realignment was still painful and fraught, but starting with a set of scores that mapped out the territory was very helpful.

A ranking/prioritizing problem also arises in conferences and workshops that must select a small number of talks or papers from a large number of submissions. There are many ways to make the selection, and the first step is generally for expert reviewers to assign a series of scores to each submission (technical merit, impact, relevance, etc.). After this step, it still falls to the event program committee to make the final selection. Though ranking scores can be used, these are often imperfect, because different reviewers review different papers and apply criteria in different ways.

Alan: *We now have review scores for all 230 papers submitted and we can accept about 15 percent, so the cutoff will be at around 35 papers."*

Stephanie: *Yes, I'd say there are about 15 with stellar scores across the board —those seem obvious to include. Then we get into a mass of about 40–50 papers which all have similar weighted averages—3–3.5 out of 5. This is going to be tough!*

Jay: *Right, I see one of the papers I reviewed and thought was pretty brilliant ended up with an average of 3.2 which would be below the cut if we just rank numerically, but frankly it's a lot more interesting than some of the middle-of-the-road stuff which ended up at 3.3 and 3.4. How accurate are these numerical scores anyway?*

Hence this is an example where a scoring approach doesn't work very well. This same problem often arises when teams take simple polls of topics where many people are not directly involved in executing the resulting decision. The votes come in with few clear winners and masses of "OK" options in the middle with middling levels of support.

One of the best ways to solve this problem is the Champion/ Detractor model, in which all program committee members are asked to assign one of four dispositions to each of the submissions that made the shortlist. Using the conference committee example:

- **Champion**: I believe it is important for this submission to be accepted and I will advocate for it.

- **Leaning Yes**: I lean toward this submission being accepted, but I will not personally advocate for it.

- **Leaning No**: I lean toward this paper being rejected, but I will not personally advocate against it.

- **Detractor**: I believe it is important for this submission not to be accepted (due to serious failings or some other serious reason) and I will advocate against its inclusion.

Generally, committee members are guided to reserve the champion status only for a relatively small number of submissions and this also happens naturally, because "Champion" is such a strong statement.

This process may seem a little esoteric; however, it proves very effective at unblocking discussion on submissions, especially when there are few slots available for success. Using only the numerical rankings often puts many submissions close together and it is hard to tell them apart.

Returning to the example above:

Alan: *Some of the papers have 'decent' scores (3.5 out of 5) from every reviewer, and some have rave reviews from some reviewers and lower scores from others.*

Stephanie: *Right, based on the scores and reviews you see, are there any which have serious flaws that maybe only one reviewer spotted? Or others which are average but have one or two really high reviews?*

Asking committee members to advocate creates an element of skin in the game and forces more clarity on which submissions are truly important (or truly flawed) versus merely generally likable. Thus a submission with just one champion is often in a better place than one that has two or three "leaning yes" votes.

This method can also be applied successfully in business decision making scenarios. At a small startup I was involved with, the team was trying to determine where to host their annual industry conference.

This was a complex optimization problem with preferences for which city to meet in, the venues available, and different dates for each location. The debate went round and round in circles with preferences unclear. Ultimately the team used the Champion-Detractor method and realized that there were really only two options people were willing to genuinely advocate for. The event ended up being held in San Francisco that year.

IN PRACTICE

1. What questions do you have about your priorities?
    1. What are the priorities in question?
    2. For each priority in question
        1. What are the opportunities gained by making each priority the highest priority?
        2. What are the risks and lost opportunities?
2. Who do you discuss your questions with, in what format, and how frequently?
3. If you want to change the dynamics of your decision process, have people either assign scores or use the Champion/Detractor model.
4. Use self-guided meditation to feel your way into each option. Stay with the guided meditation until each option takes over your body.
5. Which of these options do you want to live with while implementing it?

COMMUNICATION BETWEEN MEETINGS: THE GLUE OF COMMUNICATION CULTURE

Good communication is not just a series of good meetings. Arguably what happens between meetings is even more important. Day-to-day interactions drive many decisions: which meetings to actually have, who to involve in them, and what attitudes might be expected from people.

In 1993, one of my clients ran a company that was at $40 million in annual revenues. A small group of national chains was interested in buying my client's system if certain specific features were added. If my client landed just two of the five possible deals, revenue would be increased by 30 percent.

The CEO, the head of sales, and the chief technology officer (CTO) met with the project team leads responsible for the next release. The CTO assured the CEO and head of sales that the new functionality could be completed in the time frame that the head of sales said was necessary to land two deals.

After the meeting, several engineering team leads came to me and said that the current architecture prohibited the functionality that was required to land any two of the deals. They said that all the engineers were afraid of the CTO, who was the father of the current architecture. He attacked anyone who suggested it might be time for a new architecture.

The engineering leads asked me to deliver this message to the CEO and head of sales. I said I would not do that, but that I would be glad to facilitate a meeting in which the engineers presented their thinking to the head of sales, the CEO, and CTO. I also offered to help them prepare for the meeting.

The senior engineers met amongst themselves, and then they met with me. We role-played what each would say. They anticipated the CTO's responses and role-played various responses in return. I had offered the same support to the CTO, but he declined. I facilitated the meeting. The engineers successfully demonstrated the limits of the current architecture, arguing that a new architecture was needed. At the next staff meeting, I said, "Many in this meeting have questions they wish answered, but they have been afraid to ask."

The CEO summarized and then inquired: "So, you just said that many people in this room have questions they would like answers to but are afraid to ask. Is that right?" Heads nodded in the affirmative. Then the CEO asked, "I would very much like to hear what folks are afraid of and what we might do to manage their fear."

One lead engineer raised his hand, was acknowledged by the CEO, and said, "Sir, we are all afraid of the CTO."

The CEO asked, "What does the CTO do that causes your fear?"

Another engineering lead said, "Any time anyone raises the idea that it is time to build a second-generation architecture, the CTO rides them for several days. It is extremely unpleasant. It has discouraged us from raising issues we consider important."

The CEO turned to the CTO and asked, "Would you mind summarizing what was just said? If you prefer, I will summarize." He did. The CTO looked shocked. He said, "I had no idea about you all being scared of me. I just thought you all agreed with me. About the operating system: the thinking you all laid out makes sense to me."

The CEO gave the engineering leads responsibility for coming up with the new operating system as fast as they can. Just as the new product was released, engineering was able to add the new functionality soon enough that the sales team could close one of the three deals.

As this case shows, between meetings, communication can be critical to getting to the right decisions. The engineering team leads might have spoken up in the first meeting, but they feared the CTO's anger. They also feared that if they challenged him, they might not be able to muster the necessary facts for their argument. Often such fear leads to poor decision making. In this case, once the engineering leads banded together, they were willing to risk the CTO's anger and even the possible loss of their jobs.

Another problem between meetings is ensuring that communication happens at all. At one startup I worked with, I found another regular agenda item quite valuable: "What has worked well since we last met? What still needs to work better? What do we do next?"

This question helped surface some issues and problems that had arisen between meetings. In particular, senior staff members were often reluctant to raise issues. They also were not always sure which issues were most important to their respective staffs. A similar dynamic played out at regular all-hands meetings: an unwillingness to raise issues when the platform was there for airing them.

After some time, the leadership team instituted an always-available web form that any employee could use either anonymously or with their name to answer three simple questions:

1. What is going really well?
2. What is going badly that I would like fixed?
3. What is something I'm confused and worried about and would like the leadership team to clarify?

Employees were encouraged to use this form whenever they wished and regularly. The resulting questions were then addressed in the next all-hands staff meeting.

These simple questions often flagged issues before they became big. They also often caught rumors amongst employees that were unfounded.

IN PRACTICE

1. Who needs to do what?
2. Who needs to communicate what to whom?
3. What possible miscommunications need to be verified and corrected?
4. What disagreements need to be addressed and then resolved?
5. Who needs to coordinate with whom, about what?

IS IT TIME TO STOP TALKING?

At the architecture firm I worked with, the partners delegated the important responsibility of staffing projects on a weekly basis to the associates. At first, three and a half hours were required to complete the process each week. Three months later, the three and a half hours became less than two hours. The associates had learned to avoid doing two things that ate up time.

One of the things they had been most prone to was lapsing into problem solving, forgetting that their meeting objective was staffing projects. This was highly tempting, because each project's issues were to some extent bound up with the question of who was working on them. The associates learned to recognize when they were problem solving, and they learned how to stop problem solving and get back to staffing projects. The other time-eater: they continued to discuss the staffing of a project after they had already agreed on how to staff it. The associates learned to recognize when they were done and it was time to move on to the next project.

Three months later, project staffing required a little less than 90 minutes. In addition to eliminating some of their time-consuming additional discussions, it appeared that two other factors were involved. The associates had grown confident in their ability to staff projects, so they spent much less time second-guessing themselves. All five acknowledged their new confidence, both individually and as a team. Their communication practices were accompanied by deeper common understanding and agreement on how to staff. Much less time was spent resolving disagreements. The disagreements that did surface, and required time to resolve, were deemed important by all.

Sometimes conversations go on longer than they should. This eats up time on the agenda, risks decisions re-opening, and, above all, frustrates participants. A good indicator that it might be time to end a conversation is when the participants start repeating themselves.

We repeat ourselves when we do not feel satisfactorily understood or agreed with. Generally, this means there is some nuance that hasn't been taken on board by others, or some insight that hasn't been acknowledged.

When a conversation seems to have reached a consensus, it can still end up continuing needlessly. For individuals, the temptation is to add one more argument to a case already won. For groups, there is a temptation to drill down into all the details, when all the details are not necessary.

When a conversation has reached an impasse, repeating oneself rarely achieves greater understanding or agreement. Repetition tends to entrench positions. In both cases, repetition is a good indicator that going around the room one more time is unhelpful. When this happens, it is valuable for someone to speak up and point out the repetitive nature of the discourse. The most straightforward way to do this is to say the words, "We're repeating ourselves, is it time to end this discussion?". This may force a pause and reflection on the current status of the topic, the decision and the meeting as a whole.

IN PRACTICE

1. In meetings, listen for repetition.
    1. If it is one person who is being repetitive, interrupt and summarize what the person said.
    2. If the person continues to repeat themselves, summarize and say, "You are repeating yourself again."
    3. If several people are repeating themselves:
        a. Interrupt and say, "I think we are repeating ourselves; I know I am. Perhaps it is time to move to the next agenda item?"
        b. Follow this up by asking, "Does anyone feel not heard?"
    4. If several people say they feel not heard, it is time to summarize more frequently what was just said.
2. When a decision seems to be made, ask someone to summarize the decision.

CELEBRATING COMMUNICATIONS SUCCESS: WAY TO GO, SALLY!

Whenever you observe behavior changes that you value, acknowledge them. Celebrate them. Whenever a teammate performs well, acknowledge and celebrate the performance.

While it seems obvious that praise and encouragement are important in a team environment, they happen very rarely in many teams. Often it is down to the leader to reinforce positively, and others feel it is not their place. There are also leaders who rarely use positive reinforcement, reserving their comments for when things go wrong.

Recently, I coached a manager who wore a perpetual scowl. Those surveyed reported always feeling uncomfortable in the manager's presence. They interpreted his scowl as "He did not like what I did," "He dislikes me," "He dislikes what we are doing." In reality, however, this had much more to do with his default facial expression than his opinion of what he was seeing. The manager began to practice holding a smile in a mirror. The instruction I gave was, "Practice until your smile becomes a habit and feels like home. Practice until your wife starts smiling back at you." Twice a day he looked in the mirror and practiced holding a smile for 20 minutes. Six weeks later, half of the 10 people interviewed noticed the absence of the manager's frown and said working with him was less hard. Six weeks after that, 8 of 10 people said it was no longer hard to work with the manager.

We video conferenced weekly for an hour. Whenever he frowned, I said, very gently, "You are frowning." Whenever he smiled, I said the following kinds of things: "It is so nice to be with you when you smile," "Your smile is so comforting," and, "I really like it when you smile."

After many meetings with many clients, I will send emails of praise for specific things done during meetings: "I really admired the way you stood up to your client. You said 'no' with sincere regret. You were firm and respectful. You smiled sadly as you said no," "The ways you responded to Jay's criticism were excellent. You summarized his criticism. Then you asked him how he would like to see you do it differently. Finally, you said you needed time to think about his feedback and you would get back to him. You sounded, and felt, calm, and you seemed curious and interested. Really excellent. An amazing performance."

In NBA playoff games the players are constantly talking to each other, cheering each other on, celebrating teammates' excellent plays, giving each other criticism and instruction. More of this could go on in work teams at all levels.

Anyone on the team can give reinforcement and encouragement of good behaviors. A small comment here and there goes a long way toward highlighting what is going well and opens opportunities for easier communication when something isn't going well.

In Practice

Objective: Cultivate the habit of celebrating actions and behavior of value.

1. Think of each member of your team.
2. Describe what each member does that you value.
3. When you think of each member's value, how do you feel?
4. Think of each team member, one at a time.
   a. How do you want your teammate to feel when receiving your celebration?
   b. What words do you say?
   c. What voice do you say it in?
   d. What gestures do you use?

5. For each member of your family, do 2 through 4.

PART IV

DEFENSIVENESS AND THE ROOTS OF OUR COMMUNICATION BEHAVIOR

Parts II and III of this book have described useful tools to communicate, tune culture, and improve process and process discipline. By themselves, these tools can provide useful steps toward improvement, and I hope they suggest ideas of what might be useful for you and your team.

When we are defensive, we are limited to only three action options: fight, flight, and freeze. Fight includes unilateral control, which excludes other participants from influencing decisions that affect them. It includes bullying, public rebuke, and interrupting. Flight includes avoidance, ambiguity, and acceptance of being interrupted. Freeze does nothing. Fight, flight, freeze are embedded in our nervous systems, specifically the sympathetic nervous system. In every situation, we have a strong, deeply rooted instinct to choose one of the three. No other option occurs to us.

There are two great challenges to replacing defensiveness with the communication tools, essential processes, and awareness, compassion, courage, relatedness, and trust. The first challenge is that we were born with fight, flight, freeze embedded in our nervous systems. We need to learn to not act on these instincts, however strongly they urge us on. The second great challenge is that the communication tools, and some of the essential processes, especially inclusive decision making, are counterintuitive. It feels wrong, or even dangerous, to use them, at first.

An important characteristic of being defensive is being unaware of our defensiveness.

Reducing defensiveness makes everything easier. The first steps are awareness of our defensiveness, acceptance of it, and then ownership of it. Awareness can be, at first, emotionally painful. When this is the case, the challenge is to sustain one's awareness, despite the pain, until acceptance comes. Coming to acceptance can be a challenge. Sustaining awareness until acceptance cultivates courage. After acceptance comes ownership of our defensiveness and a commitment to replace it. At first, awareness comes after the action. Next, awareness comes during action, Then comes awareness before the action, blocking a defensive action.

How central defensiveness is became clear to me a few years ago. A dear friend from graduate school, Anne, fought with her husband for the first eight years of their marriage. Finally, Anne asked her meditation teacher for advice. The meditation teacher said, "When you start to fight, say to your husband, 'You are right.'" Anne said that it took her more than nine months to use the advice. She said that every time she thought of telling her husband that he was right, she almost threw up. She discovered how deeply ingrained was her need to be right. She started saying, "You're right," regularly. Right away, she saw how relieved her husband was and how relieved she was to avoid fighting. Within a year they fought much less frequently. Within three years, my friend says, they fought almost not at all. To top off the payoff, after three years her husband would acknowledge when he thought he was not right.

That was deeply healing for my friend. Often, her husband

would in fact not be right and would acknowledge this in the calmer discussion which followed. In changing her behavior, Anne had also affected the behavior of her husband.

Deeply ingrained habits can be overcome and replaced with good ones. The need to be right is just one example of defensiveness rearing its head in communication. My friend felt a threat from not being considered right and her responses were characteristic of the need to aggressively defend the territory of being right.

Correcting this required first having the awareness that it was going on.

To cultivate awareness requires suffering emotional pain until one says to oneself, "I am making these errors and causing these results. This is me. I am doing it." Continuing to observe ourselves despite pain requires courage and trust. We need the courage to sustain self-reflection despite our pain. We must trust that the pain will result in increased awareness that is worth it. As members of teams, we must also trust that discussion of awareness and pain does not put one's place in the team at risk.

Of course, defensiveness is not always negative. There are times when we need to be cautious, or we need to be assertive. The deep-rooted mechanism is there for a reason. However, defensiveness is extremely problematic because it is so often activated unconsciously.

Part IV begins with a deep exploration of defensiveness and descriptions of prevalent defensive behaviors, followed by a section consisting of tools to enhance awareness of self and reduce stress, especially under conditions of high stress. Next comes a discussion of the psychoanalytic definition of relatedness, which is a key component of excellent leadership. Then come sections on courage, compassion, and trust, all essential individual characteristics for excellent team participation.

- Section 1: Defensiveness: The biggest obstacle to excellence

- Section 2: Enhancing awareness: of self and others
- Section 3: Relatedness: I will not put myself above the team
- Section 4: Courage: Taking right action when facing fear
- Section 5: Compassion: Replacing judgment with empathy and right action
- Section 6: Trust: Do you trust me? Do I trust you?

Defensiveness: The insidious scourge of teams

The dictionary defines defensiveness as, "being anxious to challenge or avoid criticism." Our definition of defensiveness is a bit more expansive, as you will see below. Almost all human social behavior is defensive. This may sound startling at first, but as we look at different behaviors we'll increasingly see the truth in it.

A Harvard–MIT research team, led by Chris Argyris and Donald A. Schon, spent over 20 years studying organizations and their behavior [Argyris and Schon, 1978]. This research was one of the things that first showed me how much more there was to communication than most standard theories covered. Argyris and Schon found that every organization they studied "responded to errors in ways that reinforced the conditions for errors." Their case studies, over and over, describe the common errors discussed in this book.

They found that defensiveness is ubiquitous and exists at every level of human organization, from the individual right through empire and beyond. The good news is that once defensiveness is owned and removed, performance explodes.

The common errors in teams they identified were as follows:

1. Issues that need to be managed better remain undiscussed in appropriate forums.

2. At all levels, action differs from intentions and plans. Many differences remain hidden, or, if known, remain undiscussed.

3. Communication is ambiguous, producing misinterpretations that in turn burn resources, slow progress, produce frustration, and strain relationships.

4. Disagreements harming teamwork remain unresolved.

5. Some team members are excluded from influencing decisions that they are responsible to implement and that are important to them.

6. Defensiveness is accompanied by unawareness of one's own defensiveness.

Some of these may have their roots in inefficiency, lack of time, or inattentiveness; but in the studies' detail it is clear that many of the errors are due to individual behaviors that limit information deliberately or unconsciously. Taboo topics, for example, often do not get discussed because of the discomfort they would cause some of the team members. Ambiguities remain because team members feel uncomfortable pointing out gaps or fully explaining their motivations.

Defensiveness places an artificially low ceiling on even the most talented team's performance. Individuals and teams tend to be aware of the defensiveness of others while remaining unaware of their own. To liberate oneself and one's team from defensiveness is a great challenge and worth the effort. Liberation from defensiveness requires awareness, courage, compassion, relatedness, and trust. Each of these will be discussed below.

When an issue is taboo, members of the team fear that raising it will jeopardize their place on the team. To raise taboo issues requires courage or trust: the courage to raise the issue in the face of fearing the loss of one's place on the team, but also trust that the team will respond positively. Liberation also requires a productive discussion of one's own and one's team's defensiveness. When we are defensive, we try to control events that affect us by editing the information we exchange with others: we leave things out, we exaggerate, we distort, and we diminish information. And we act as if we are not doing these things.

In the age before computers, I coached an engineering supervisor named Harry in the data storage company I've called Harpers. He said to me, "Al is the best engineer I have. His drawings are perfect. But he produces half the work of any other engineer. When he is at his desk, he is usually on a personal call. When he is not at his desk, he is usually at the water cooler flirting with the secretaries."

I asked, "Have you talked to him about your criticisms?"

Harry said, "I did."

I followed up, "Say to me what you said to Al. Say it as if I am Al."

Harry said, "Al you do great work, but you have to improve your citizenship."

I summarized, "You just told Al that he has to improve his citizenship. Did I hear you clearly?" Harry said yes.

I asked, "Did he do anything different after that?"

Harry said, "He started wearing a tie to work."

This was not the desired outcome. I summarized, to Harry's satisfaction, what he had said about Al's performance. I then said, "For Al to have a chance to improve his performance in the ways you want him to, you need to say to him what you said to me."

Harry said, "Oh, I could never say those things to Al. It would be rude."

I said, "What is rude about describing to Al the things he needs to do differently to keep his job?"

"It would make him feel bad. I was taught you never make another person feel bad."

I asked Harry, "As manager of your department, what is your responsibility to the company?"

"To make sure we get all of our work done, on time, to the right quality and specification, within budget."

How does Al's performance reflect on your own performance?"

"Not well."

"I think you have a dilemma. "To do my job, I must be rude. To avoid being rude also inhibits the performance of my job. What do you think, Harry?"

"Sounds right. I am stuck."

I agreed with Harry that it is a place where many of us get stuck.

"You need to decide, I think, which is more important to you," I suggested. "Being polite and not telling Al what he needs to improve, or being rude and giving him a chance to improve?"

Harry: "I think I need to suck it up, and talk with Al."

Harry met with Al. Harry said, "Al, you do the best drawings, but your productivity is low. You need to double the number of drawings you do in a week. You need to be at your desk working at nine. You must reduce the time you spend on personal calls at your desk." By the end of the next year, Al was producing more drawings than the engineering department's average. He became Harry's top performer.

In this case, the supervisor's defensiveness and unwillingness to violate politeness put an employee at risk. This type of situation arises again and again in team settings: by avoiding conflict and ducking what might be an unpleasant interaction, we often put someone more at risk than if we had that hard conversation.

It can get much worse when more than a job is at stake. This is a case of subordinates withholding information for fear their superior does not want to hear it. During the presidency of Gerald Ford, the swine flu epidemic occurred. Ford held a meeting with scientists at the White House. A vaccine had been developed, but the test results were unclear. Many of the scientists at the meeting had privately expressed doubts about the efficacy and safety of the vaccine. But, to a person, they believed that the President wanted their approval for distributing the vaccine. The president asked to hear any concerns the scientists had about the vaccine and its distribution. Not one scientist spoke up. The vaccine was distributed. Unfortunately, the vaccine resulted in over 450 people developing the paralyzing Guillain-Barré syndrome, a rare neurological disorder (*New York Times*, Sept. 2, 2020: "Gerald Ford Rushed Out a Vaccine. It Was a Fiasco").

Our instinct in communication is to avoid fear and pain, especially in the near term, both for ourselves and the listener. Unfortunately, this often means important messages are not voiced or heard.

Defensiveness also often takes another form: offense or distraction. When a speaker is worried about a truth, a conversation, or a given decision, the speaker may choose to throw out other topics like a screen of chaff to cover the issue they would rather not discuss. This form of deflection can range from being unreasonable on another agenda point to evading questions and answering with generalities to gloss over key issues.

In one example I witnessed, some members of the board of a large food cooperative had come to believe that the organization lacked the management depth to operate both a wholesale produce operation and a retail operation. Other board members were deeply committed to continuing to own and run both operations. Whenever a board member raised the issue of selling or closing one or the other operation, one of two things happened: either a board member would get angry and attack the board member who raised the issue, or, once the issue was raised, other board members deflected discussion by redirecting the conversation to other issues.

The defensiveness that drives so much of our communications style is ingrained in us. It is often our default, unconscious mode of operating when we are thinking about upcoming conversations.

The previous sections of the book have already outlined a number of tools to unlock ourselves and others from some of the traps in which defensiveness catches us. However, to go further we really need to dig deeper into a set of broader practices that help us tackle defensiveness itself.

These practices can be broadly categorized:

- Awareness practices: knowing what one is doing in communication. Watching videos of oneself during meetings, asking others what you do well and what they would like to see you do better or different.

- Analysis practices: understanding where the defensiveness comes from and what effects it has; becoming aware of the thoughts, emotions, internal narratives, postures, motions, and breath that accompanies your defensiveness

- Corrective measures: taking action to change communication patterns when they are detected.

The rest of Part IV will cover techniques in each of these categories. We begin with awareness and analysis to comprehensively understand the situation and then cover selflessness, courage, compassion, and trust as corrective measures.

IN PRACTICE

Raising previously avoided issues publicly:

1. List the issues your team needs to manage better but which are avoided in the appropriate team forums.
2. Form a two-column case.
   a. The left column is for everything uttered out loud by any participant in the discussion.
   b. The right column is for everything you are thinking and feeling and not uttering publicly.
3. Score your two-column case.

a. For both columns, underline statements relevant to the issue being discussed.

b. For both columns circle judgmental statements.

c. Count how many relevant issues are in the right-hand column and not in the left?

d. Relevant issues in the right (private) column indicate defensiveness.

e. The existence of private judgment is defensive.

4. Imagine articulating the relevant thoughts that you have kept private.

a. What would you say?

b. What bad thing are you concerned will happen if you say a.?

c. What data do you have that suggests this bad thing might happen?

Identifying the common symptoms of defensiveness produced by your team

For your convenience, the common symptoms are repeated just below. Note which symptoms you observe on your own teams.

1. Issues that need to be better managed remain undiscussed in appropriate forums.

2. At all levels, action differs from intentions and plans. The differences remain hidden, or, if known, remain undiscussed.

3. Miscommunication burns resources, slows progress, produces frustration, and strains relationships.

4. Disagreements harming teamwork remain unresolved.

5. Some team members are excluded from influencing decisions that are important to them.

6. Some decisions remain unmade.

7. There is competition for influence, resources, and opportunities.

8. The completion of important tasks is predictably, precariously late.

9. Defensiveness is always accompanied by unawareness of one's own defensiveness.

AWARENESS OF SELF AND OTHERS

Awareness affords us knowledge and perception of something that happened. It is knowledge of an occurrence. The occurrence may have been something within oneself (a feeling, an emotion), something acted upon (making a statement) or something someone else did. The awareness can also come right at the time when the event is happening or, in some cases, many years afterwards. Awareness is a powerful tool.

Awareness after something has occurred can sometimes feel useless, leading to thoughts of what one might have said differently if one had been aware enough at the time. It is still valuable because it can teach us how to act differently next time.

Awareness-in-the-moment is knowledge and perception of the moment. In the moment, we know what is happening. Sometimes we may even slow down enough to prevent some instinctive reaction from taking over our voice and saying something we will later regret. Even if we don't, we may be able to follow up in a way that acknowledges our error.

Awareness of others is also very powerful. How is Sam reacting to Sally's presentation? Is Jim sold on the proposal I just made? Our sense of how people react may not always be accurate, but often we can get key insights into how others are feeling by being more aware of what is happening in a room.

Awareness of self begets awareness of others because we can know of others only what we know of ourselves. Cultivating awareness is a great challenge. It requires the discovery of how our actions differ from our plans and intentions. These discoveries are often accompanied by emotional discomfort—in many cases shame, guilt, or self-loathing. But the only way to greater awareness is through pain. This requires courage and trust that the effort will prove beneficial.

Awareness and communication go hand in hand. To improve communication, we must increase our awareness. Here are the elements of communication that it pays to increase awareness of:

- What we say, word for word (verbatim)
- The voice we use
- The face we display
- The posture we hold
- The gestures we make
- Our thoughts
- Our emotions and bodily sensations
- Our impact on others
- The impact of others on others

At first glance, when presented with this list, most people would say, "Of course, I am aware of these things." However, as we have already been discovering, we are often very poor at perceiving what is happening in a conversation. In many cases we would even be unable to repeat what has just been said. Surprisingly, it is the same for what we ourselves say.

Our Limited Set of Interpersonal Patterns

Each of us has a limited set of interpersonal patterns that consist of our verbatim utterances, specific voice, face, posture, gestures, breath, thoughts, emotions, bodily sensations, and effect on others. In each of our patterns we take one of four positions: we lead, follow, oppose, or observe. We have a different interpersonal pattern for each. We have distinct interpersonal patterns for elation, fear, joy, collaboration, competition, etc. This comes, first, from David

Kantor and Will Lehr (2003). My own work with clients validates their findings.

Awareness-in-the-moment does not require that we monitor all these elements at the same time. Once we know a pattern, we can monitor one or two of its elements to be aware of ourselves in the moment. For example, when I am aggressive, I lean forward. I point with the first finger of my left hand. My voice feels like a growl and sounds that way to others. My face looks angry. My throat is so tense it aches. My shoulders are tight. My neck feels stiff. My language is filled with judgments, and so are my thoughts. The effect is intimidating, sometimes hurtful and insulting, never good for me.

I learned to monitor my throat and shoulders. When they got tense, I learned to lean back, put the top of my back on the back of the chair, place my hands in my lap, and with each exhale, release tension in my throat and shoulders. The leaning back and placing my hands in my lap interrupted my defensive behavior. Releasing tension in my throat and shoulders reduced my stress so I no longer felt aggressive.

Now, in my 70s, I have cultivated an interpersonal pattern of friendliness. I smile. I nod greetings. I always gesture for the other person to go before me. There is little tension in my body. My throat glows with warmth. My thoracic cavity is alight with love. People smile back at me.

In the past, the aggressive stance often came on unbidden when I was irked by a small detail in something. This negativity often meant the words I said had very different outcomes than those I intended. The ability to stay friendly despite the odd annoyance has made a huge change to my interactions with others. More importantly, it is often a much better reflection of what I want to convey. There are cases where an aggressive stance is warranted, but even here my practice of friendliness brings benefits: when people see a stance I rarely use, they sit up and take notice.

Awareness of Others

There is a set of elements we can observe in others. We can hear their verbatim (word for word) utterances; we can hear and physically experience their voices. Voice is the invisible force that touches us emotionally in ways we are unaware of. We can observe the faces, postures, and movements of others. All of these affect us. Often, we are unaware of the impact these elements have on us. The more self-aware we become, the more we can be aware of others and their impact.

It has been helpful to me to cultivate my ability to observe these elements one or two at a time. My first efforts focused on what was said, word for word (verbatims) and the voices of myself and others. Once I began cultivating my ability to observe one or two elements, I asked the question, over and over, "If I was saying those words in that voice, what might I be thinking, feeling, hoping for, trying to avoid, and concerned about?" Any element can be used to ask this question, and sometimes, what we need to be aware of is what is not expressed in words. What follows is an example.

The head of engineering was listing the new functionality going into the next release. I noticed the head of marketing shake his head, ever so slightly, staring down at the table. When the head of engineering was done talking there was silence. I waited for the head of marketing to say something, expecting a disagreement with something the head of engineering had listed or left out. I asked the head of marketing what he thought about engineering's list. He said that engineering had left off the list the function asked for by every customer and prospect. Discussion revealed an important difference in the data held by engineering and that held by marketing. Once this difference in data was uncovered, the general manager said that he would visit several customers recommended by engineering and several recommended by marketing.

After two visits, the general manager understood the difference in the data sets. Engineering was talking to the IT folks. Marketing was talking with the executives who made the buy decisions. On the discovery of this difference, the functionality wanted by marketing was put at the top of engineering's list. Then the head of engineering turned to the head of marketing and asked him what functionality should be removed from the list.

Later, the head of marketing said that he had decided not to raise his disagreement. He said that he was tired of trying to influence engineering. The moral of this story is the power of awareness. Marketing's slight head shake was easy to miss; had I not noticed it, I would probably have asked the table, "What do you think?" and everyone would probably have accepted the silence from the head of marketing.

This is a basic empathy exercise. I asked myself the question until it became a habit—a useful habit.

IN PRACTICE

1. When listening, be as still and as quiet as you can be.
2. When listening, do not talk to yourself.
3. Let other people's voices play on your body as the wind does on a wind chime.
4. Observe the physical sensations that arise within you.
5. Practice steps 1–4 until they become habits.
6. When listening, do not look at the speaker, look at those around the table.
7. Observe the nonverbal responses to what is being said.
8. When talking, observe those who are listening; scan for strong nonverbal responses.
9. When appropriate, ask the person with a strong nonverbal response what he or she thought about what you said.
10. In meetings, observe the posture of those around the table.
11. What do you surmise each posture might tell you about what each person is thinking and feeling?

RELATEDNESS: I WILL NOT PUT MYSELF FIRST

The dictionary definition (Webster's Third New International Dictionary, Unabridged,1963) of relatedness is:

the fact of being connected with something/somebody in some way.
the sense of relatedness and interdependence of all life.

Relatedness is a broad term used in a variety of contexts; the meaning closest to our purposes comes from psychoanalytic theory, specifically, Wilfrid Bion's "Experiences in Groups" (1991): "the avoidance of placing one's own interests above others, under stress." All the best leaders I have coached and consulted to have demonstrated relatedness, consistently. They never put their own interests above those of their teams. When a leader does this, morale is fortified. It is a professional blessing to be led by leaders who never put their own interests above the team.

Relatedness has powerful effects.

For a law firm I consulted, I facilitated an annual partner meeting. At the meeting, the partners allocated a percentage of the year's profits among themselves. Several years in a row, one of the two senior partners gave away significant percentage points to other partners. The second year he did this, he and I were driving back from the meeting, and I expressed my deep appreciation for his humanity and generosity. He got angry with me. He harrumphed, and said, "That was not generosity or humanity. That was just sound business."

Later, at the architectural firm, when Bernice, Jim, and Denny formed their partnership, Bernice insisted on taking half the amount of the ownership taken by Jim and Denny. Everyone tried to help Bernice see that she was making a big mistake. She stuck to her guns, took half, and 18 months later was experiencing resentment about having half of what her partners had.

Bernice was the moral center of the firm. She tried as hard as she could to avoid her resentment leaking into the firm, but leak it did. The founders advocated making Bernice an equal partner. They offered all their remaining shares, but this fell short of equal. At first, Jim and Denny resisted. They resented having to give up any shares at this point. The founders helped Jim and Denny see that it was an essential gesture for the ongoing health and morale of the firm.

When the new distribution agreement was announced to the staff, almost everyone stood and cheered. A year later both Jim and Denny expressed relief at having avoided a terrible decision and gratitude for the founders' help in seeing what was needed.

To develop or cultivate relatedness requires high commitment and high self-awareness. When cultivating relatedness, it helps to experience exemplary models. Developing self-awareness of the conditions under which we put our own interests above the interests of the team or of a teammate is essential. Then develop by experimenting with the use of rules that enable you to avoid placing your own interests above the team's under stress. Practice the new rules until they become second nature and habitual.

One of the firms I worked with (named Bennett Electronics for the purposes of this book), was searching for a new CMO. Their first product was not gaining traction. The CMO had been fired, and the company had not found a good replacement. The executive team was feeling desperate. Then they came upon an excellent candidate. They made him an offer that he refused. He said that he was already CMO of a bigger company and it would make little sense to move because it would be a step down. The candidate said he would be happy to join the team, but only as CEO.

With no hesitation, Jim, the current CEO, offered to step aside. This was by no means easy for Jim. He loved being CEO. He did not want to give it up. And he worried about what he would do with his time. However, he stepped aside with no hesitation. He said, "We need him more than we need me. Besides, I would rather be rich than CEO." The new CEO changed the marketing strategy, and their IPO was the biggest ever.

Sacrifices do not need to be this big to be effective; however, relatedness requires members of the team to be attuned to each other's needs and the needs of the team and to have a good understanding of what each is willing to do for the team.

Relatedness builds on awareness and encourages team members to act on behalf of the team. It may often feel very difficult to live up to the high standard of putting the group above oneself, especially when others are not doing the same. Small steps often begin the culture change process. Being one of the first gets the ball rolling and offers encouragement to others to follow the way.

IN PRACTICE

1. Who on the team, under what conditions, avoids placing their own interests above the team's interests?
    1. What did the teammates do to avoid placing their interests above the team's?
    2. What good does this bring to the team?
    3. Does the good warrant action, such as recognition and celebration?
    4. What forum should this be raised in?
    5. Verbatim write down what should be said.
2. Who on the team, under what conditions, places their own interests above the team's interests?
    1. What did the teammates do to place their interests above the team's?
    2. What harm does this bring to the team?
    3. Does the harm warrant action?
    4. What forum should this be raised in?
    5. Verbatim write down what should be said.
    6. Verbatim write down what teammates will say in response?

COURAGE: TAKING THE RIGHT ACTION WHEN FACED WITH FEAR

Courage is not fearlessness. Courage is the ability to take right action, with all necessary effort, when experiencing fear. Courage is needed to raise difficult issues. Courage is needed to give critical performance feedback. Courage is needed to receive critical performance feedback productively.

During my academic career, I was one of four teaching fellows for the fall semester Organization Behavior 101A at the Harvard Graduate School of Education. Bill Torbert was the professor leading the class. It was the middle of October, and the trees were starting to show their fall colors. At the end of class, I said, "Papers are due next week." Three or four students tried to correct me by saying that papers were due in two weeks. I insisted it was next week. Class was on Mondays. The next Sunday night I got a call from the professor who said, "You are at risk of losing your class." I was wrong. Papers were due in two weeks, not one. Some students had canceled their reservations at country inns where they wanted to see the fall colors.

During our meeting with the professor, before the Monday class, I expressed terror at facing my class. At the end of the meeting, I sat stuck in my chair. I felt like I could not get up. Finally, the professor said, "If you are not going into that classroom, I am." That got me up and moving. I went into class, sat down, and said, "I made a terrible mistake. I am very sorry. I would like to hear each of your individual complaints." After each person shared their complaint, I summarized and apologized directly. After class was over, I was mobbed with congratulations for the courage with which I handled the situation. Experiencing this, I committed myself to always own my mistakes before those who were affected by them.

As I have mentioned before, the actions prescribed in this book are counterintuitive. They require us to act in ways that violate ubiquitous defensive norms. For many of us, the anticipation of violating norms, even with the best of intentions, raises our stress level, which many of us experience as fear. Thus, courage is needed to implement the prescribed actions of this book, at least at first. Later, once these behaviors become second nature, they are easier.

Many of the interpersonal issues that arise in the work environment can feel deeply uncomfortable. They can range from awkward, unpleasant news that must be communicated, to addressing mistakes, to the fear of losing one's place in the group. It takes courage to face these situations and address them rather than letting them fester and grow more intransigent over time. It is almost always worth addressing difficult situations. Discussing difficult issues well builds morale. Discussing difficult issues well builds trust that they can be successfully addressed. This reduces the fear of raising them.

IN PRACTICE

1. Prepare for a conversation that requires courage.

2. Write down what you must say and what you must ask. Write the words as you would say them to the other person.

3. Write what you imagine the other person will say out loud, and what s/he will be thinking and feeling, but not saying.

4. Role-play with another person what you say in 2 and what the other person says in 3.

5. Role-play repeatedly, until what you say feels as if it is second nature to you. In particular, try to role play with a second trusted person. Having this second person involved will help make the role-play much more real.

TRUST: BELIEVING ANOTHER WILL DO THE RIGHT THING

You trust someone to be on time, to deliver on time what you expected her or him to deliver. Having trustworthy teammates is a relief, a comfort. When I rely on someone whom I do not find trustworthy, I spend time and energy wondering whether the person will deliver what I need when I need it. When I work with someone I find trustworthy, I spend no time or energy worrying about the deliverable. Trustworthiness saves energy by causing less worry.

The absence of trustworthiness can cause stress and interpersonal tension. The more important the task the untrustworthy person, or team, is responsible for, the higher the stress and tension.

When motivated, teammates can learn to improve their trustworthiness with timely, sufficiently specific feedback.

In a team, trust is a firm belief in the trustworthiness of each teammate. Trust is always accompanied by a dramatic reduction in stress. Trust makes everything easier. Trust is built upon the trustworthiness of each teammate. And here, as usual, is the rub: We humans tend to remain unaware of the ways in which we are not trustworthy. Increased trust requires awareness of the ways in which we are not trustworthy. Awareness requires seeing clearly what we do and the unintended consequences of what we do. This tends to increase stress. Developing awareness requires staying focused under high stress.

Feel your way into each of the following team conditions regarding trust:

1. Every teammate confidently relies on every other teammate to do their job well and deliver, on time, what the plan requires.

2. One teammate causes worry to all the other teammates.

3. Teammates worry about each other.

How does each condition feel? Condition 1 is the most satisfying emotional experience. It is the kind of experience that strengthens one's heart physically and spiritually if one has such a spiritual bent. Condition 1 is accompanied by the highest possible productivity and morale. Condition 1 is a rare condition. Most teams are condition 2 or condition 3. Thank goodness that more teams are condition 2 than condition 3. Teams in condition 2 succeed much more often than teams in condition 3. In fact, teams in condition 3 rarely succeed.

The marketing department at Bennett Electronics moved from condition 3 to condition 1. Recall that the CMO was fired. He was untrustworthy. He had never clarified roles and responsibilities. Disputes over overlapping responsibilities were endless. The situation was demoralizing for everyone in the department. Stan, Bennett's new CEO, was also operating as CMO. Stan then named Grace as his chief operating officer for marketing. He gave Grace carte blanche to reorganize as she saw fit. She did. Everyone was clear about their roles and responsibilities, including who had to deliver what to whom, in what state of completion, by when. Collaboration sprung up all around the department. But there still was one key member of the marketing team who was still untrustworthy, Harley, head of field marketing. Grace organized a meeting to give Harley feedback. Harley received the feedback by summarizing each teammate's feedback. Then, receiving feedback weekly from the team, he became increasingly trustworthy over the next three months.

Team leaders must be accountable for their trustworthiness. When leaders are trustworthy, and when they hold each teammate accountable, condition 1 occurs.

For years I worked with a Wall Street trading firm that made markets on the New York Stock Exchange (NYSE). I spent many days on the trading floor. It took only a couple of days to realize that the NYSE's trading system was based on trust. The buying and selling takes place face to face in a room that goes from very quiet to very noisy and back again. The broker and the market maker (called a "specialist") agree on the number of shares being exchanged at a specific price. When I was there, oh so many years ago, the brokers and specialists wrote their exchanges down on small white pads, in pencil. Misunderstandings and disagreements were rare.

Trust given creates a reciprocal bond that is hard to break. There is strength not only in being trusted by someone but also in the act of trusting. Trust is built on relatedness, compassion, and, of course, a sense of the reliability of the person being trusted. At a deeper level, trust also takes courage: it takes courage on the part of the person placing their trust (they are taking a risk) and on the part of the person accepting that trust (they are putting their skills and reputation on the line to be able to do something).

In another case, Ralph was heading up the new corporate systems lab, chartered with designing one operating system to be used by all products from all three business units. It was discovered that the executives from all three business units hated Ralph. They said he was rude and insulting. They deeply mistrusted him. For the past three years, Ralph had led the systems lab for the highest revenue business unit. Every year the executives shrank Ralph's budget. It was also discovered that Ralph was beloved in all three systems labs.

Ralph was told that the executives hated and mistrusted him. He accepted the information. He talked to those he was close to. They described his rudeness and arrogance when communicating with the executives. He owned what he did.

He went to the executives and told them what he had learned. He apologized and asked for examples. He summarized and asked follow-up questions. Then he changed his behavior. He learned to engage the executives as he did those in the systems labs, with humor, humility, and really good listening.

At the end of the lab's first fiscal year, the business units gave the lab more money than it had asked for. To a person, the executives voiced pleasure in working with Ralph. Many said how much they now trusted him.

Trust is a wonderful thing; it deepens and enlivens the flow of planning, deciding, implementing, operating, and supervising. Not only is a feeling of trust an important part of the "safety" people must feel when communicating in a team, it also means a lot less detail is needed in some discussions because one or more of the team members are trusted to take care of the details. In team communications in particular, trust is the highest currency.

Trust should not be granted lightly. Trust should be earned. We need to be discerning about those to whom we grant trust. A common error is trusting in someone, or something, that should not be trusted. At a project early in my career, a plant manager trusted me. I did not know what I was doing. I gave him an instruction that unintentionally shut down the plant for two days. I may have been trustworthy on the communication topics I worked on with the team, but for operational issues I was not trustworthy. I had not yet acknowledged to myself my operational incompetence.

There are no real shortcuts to building trust in a team. Awareness, relatedness, and courage are required to build trust. These are what form the basis of beliefs like "Jackie says she'll take the task and she'll not only deliver but do it well." There are really only trust-building and trust-breaking activities. Almost every interaction in a group, team or one-to-one relationship is either one or the other.

Some examples of trust-building interactions include:

- Listening well and showing others they are understood
- Discussing difficult issues productively
- Solving a tough problem together
- Being playful in kind ways; in other words, teasing only with an open heart
- Having fun together
- Everyone doing what they commit to
- Everyone owning their own errors
- Acknowledgement and celebration of good results

- Holding each other accountable

Examples of things that break trust:

- Making decisions without all stakeholders in the loop
- Ignoring comments made by a team member
- Not delivering on a commitment
- Ignoring a contribution made or taking credit for someone else's work
- Changing plans without regard for the negative impact on others in the team
- Participants attempting to prove themselves right and others wrong

Some of the positive reinforcements are clearly about awareness, relatedness, and courage, or competence and reliability, rather than trust itself. However, these items build trust because they all illustrate willingness in the group to engage with each other.

IN PRACTICE

1. Ask your teammates to describe the ways in which you are:
    1. Trustworthy
    2. Not trustworthy
    3. Ask your teammates about the
    4. Value of your trustworthiness
    5. The cost of your lack of trustworthiness
    6. Ask your teammates what they want you to do differently.
    7. For each teammate, describe what they do that is:
    8. Trustworthy
    9. Untrustworthy
2. Describe what you would like each to do differently.

COMPASSION: REPLACING JUDGMENT WITH EMPATHY AND ACTION

Webster's dictionary defines compassion as: "sympathetic pity and concern for the sufferings or misfortunes of others." The Buddhist author Sharon Salzberg offers what I consider a powerful alternative definition: "Compassion is to take right action, with all necessary effort, while responding to suffering and injustice with empathy." This comes from her book *Lovingkindness* (2020). As with relatedness, this is a more action-oriented definition of compassion, implying that compassion compels us to act.

Compassion, at its root, starts with the more widely understood notion of empathy, "the ability to understand and share the feelings of another." When we are empathic, we see more of other people than we see when we are in judgment. One can cultivate empathy, which is the ability to understand and share the feelings of others. Deep empathy requires deep self-knowledge. We can only know of others what we know of ourselves.

Empathy is the act of transposing oneself into the situation of someone else. What might I be thinking if I said and did what she said and did? What does it feel like to wear the other person's postures and movements? What emotions might you be experiencing in the moment? What does it feel like to wear the other person's face? As empathy becomes a habit, the next challenge is to sustain it under increasing stress.

General Motors (GM) was founded by William C. Durant. In 1918, facing a severe economic recession, J P Morgan and Company, the Dupont Corporation (which had just invested heavily in GM), and Durant entered into a secret agreement to support the stock price of General Motors. They believed, "As goes General Motors, so goes the broader market." The agreement included a covenant that no individual involved in the secret agreement could buy the stock for their own account. Durant violated the covenant and bought the stock for his own account. In consequence, he went broke and the purchase threatened the stock price of GM and the market as a whole.

The Duponts and Morgans redoubled their efforts to support the GM stock price. They also bailed Durant out and let him keep $7 million. Durant used this money to start Durant Motor Car Company, which went belly up not long after it was founded. Durant was stone cold broke. He was old and his body was broken. Annually, until the death of Durant's widow, Alfred Sloan, CEO of GM, took up a collection from all the GM millionaires to support Durant and his wife. This shows not only empathy for Durant and his family but compassion and follow-through to real action to do something about the situation. Sloan was heard to say, "If Durant had not put all the pieces together, there would be no General Motors, and none of us would be this rich. We owe him, even if he did not keep his word. I have put myself, imaginatively, in Mr. Durant's shoes, and it is a very uncomfortable place to be. We have the ability to remove some of his discomfort, and so we do."

Compassion begins with empathy. Get to know your teammates empathically. Observe their actions. Begin by considering things a teammate does that you respect, admire, or value. Wonder what you might be thinking and feeling if you were taking the action you just observed. You might say something such as, "I admire the way you do that. I wondered what I would be thinking if I did what you did. Here is what I thought... What do you think?"

When you see a teammate down on herself or discouraged, encourage them. But do so only sincerely. Avoid insincerity. Cheer successes. Acknowledge commitment and hard work.

In Practice

Waking up your empathy

1. Think of someone you love.
2. Recall a time this person you love expressed happiness.
3. Continue to recall the experience of this loved one expressing happiness. Do this until it takes over your body.
4. Describe how you feel experiencing your loved one's happiness.
5. Think of this same loved one in pain.
6. Continue to recall this experience of your loved one in pain. Do this until it takes over your body.
7. Describe how you feel experiencing your loved one in pain.

Seeing compassion in others

1. Identify someone you think is compassionate.
2. Think of a time you experienced this person acting with compassion.
3. Describe what the person does that expresses compassion.
4. Repeat 1–3 with several other people.
5. What do they have in common when acting with compassion?
6. What habits of compassion do you want to cultivate?

Preparing for compassionate action

1. Think of a difficult conversation coming up that is likely to cause more pain and discomfort to another participant in the conversation.
2. Write what you must say that will cause the other participants pain and discomfort.

3. Now try to put yourself in the other person's place and imagine hearing/receiving what you plan to say. Keep imagining until the imagining takes over your body. This is your empathic body for this situation. In our empathic body, we can experience what it is like to be in the body of another, what the other is feeling emotional.

4. Describe your empathic body. Where are you holding tension in your body? What does that tension feel like?

5. When having the actual conversation put on the empathic body you described in 4.

PART V

INTO THE VIRTUAL

In 2020, the COVID-19 pandemic made remote work dramatically more prevalent than before, increasing its frequency in companies that already used it and leading many teams to work virtual for the first time. Many of the fundamentals discussed in this book still very much apply in this pandemic changed world and are even amplified by the shift to virtual. Others are changing subtly.

I have been working with some clients virtually since 1989 when it was done by phone. I have been working via videoconferencing for almost 20 years. For the past 15 years, I have been working with virtual teams and companies.

Both the face-to-face work world and the virtual work world produce in equal amounts the common errors we listed at the beginning of the book. In both worlds, high morale, first-class communication, and collaboration can be achieved but are difficult. In a virtual organization, there are no encounters in the hallway, at the coffee maker, or at the water cooler. It can be harder for people to listen and understand one another. Everything must also be scheduled. On the other hand, short check-in meetings carry less cost and can be more frequent. Being at home rather than in a crowded office can also lead to more productive time.

In this part of the book, we'll take some of the key concepts we've already covered and work through how they change in this new virtual world. The text is divided as follows:

- Five Types of Meetings
- Virtual as an Individual
- Virtual as a Team
- Virtual Culture.

FIVE TYPES OF MEETINGS

Different types of meetings are affected differently by the move to a virtual environment. Here they are classified into five types:

- **Presentations**: one or a small number of speakers presenting content to a (typically) larger number of viewers and listeners.

- **One-on-ones**: typically, two individuals, where each person is expected to contribute roughly equally to the conversation.

- **Group discussions**: three or more individuals coming together to investigate a topic, make a decision, or otherwise exchange views, where everybody in the meeting has an opinion and/or voice on the topic at hand and is expected to make some contribution.

- **Virtual watercoolers**: socially focused gatherings with no set work agenda that aim to spark closer connection among team members and serendipitous exchange of ideas.

- **Spontaneous meetings**: small meetings of two to three people that are not preplanned but arise on demand to resolve one or a small number of very focused issues.

Each of the meeting types will be discussed in detail below, and in the sections following these, we'll dive into specific techniques that can help improve each meeting type.

Presentations

Presentations were the most common form of online meetings prior to the recent rapid growth of online meetings. In presentations, a single presenter or perhaps a small team is delivering content to some other group. That group could be small (even one person) but it's typically rather larger—team of three, four, or more, or even an audience of hundreds or thousands.

The biggest difference between online and in-person presentations that presenters bring up is the difficulty in connecting with and engaging with the audience. It can be very difficult to know whether people are even listening, let alone whether or how they are reacting to content. This is particularly true if as a presenter you have slides or other materials to show on screen, because your own screen is likely dominated by this content and not by any kind of view of the audience. Worse, the audience may have many more distractions in their immediate vicinity than they had before.

On the positive side, if the audience is paying attention, they can probably see the speaker and the content much more clearly than in a large room. It is also much easier to record the meeting for later review, and there can be a lot of value in having chat, Q&A, and other audience participation functions alongside the presentation

One-on-Ones

Unexpectedly, one-on-one meetings might be the type of meeting which changes the least between physical and virtual variants. There is clearly a loss of fidelity, in that reactions can be harder to perceive and socially pleasant elements of the experience, such as being in a nice place, are lost. However, in a one-on-one context both participants are likely to be focused on the conversation itself, and if cameras are used, then, as we'll discuss below, there is still a tremendous amount of emotion that can be transmitted.

In such settings, sensitive topics will still raise emotions. Without the other physical cues, we all also tend to tune in more to facial expressions and tone of voice. Sometimes this can lead to more misunderstandings, but with good regular contact, these can be minimized.

There are also advantages in that one-on-one virtual meetings can be less time-consuming and easier to schedule. There's no walking to and from a desk or to another building, for example. For some shy people, virtual meetings of this type may also be preferable; they are in a more comfortable private environment and feel they have more control over how they appear than in a physical space.

One more change that remains problematic, however, is that people may perceive a virtual one-on-one as less "valuable" and, hence, as a sign of disrespect. This very much depends on whether a physical option was even possible and on whether people are treating the meeting seriously. However, for important topics it is important to ensure that there is enough formality in the way the meeting is scheduled, where participants are, that they arrive on time, so that the other party does not perceive the meeting to be of lower value than it ought to be.

Group Discussions

Discussion-type meetings with multiple people coming together to sift through ideas or make a complex decision are perhaps the hardest type of meeting to have virtually. They combine elements of presentation, rapid back-and-forth discussion, and reaching decisions, with far-reaching effects on the team. There may also be significant negative effects if one or more of the stakeholders at the meeting doesn't feel heard or represented in the decisions taken.

Some of the most challenging aspects of the team discussion as a virtual meeting include:

- Establishing a way of delivering information and opinions that doesn't slip into a long presentation mode in which only one participant is talking.

- Ensuring that those who have an opinion or idea can voice it, while avoiding being sidetracked by every new idea.

- Gauging the level of engagement of participants and their level of interest in or support for each of the ideas being discussed.

- Moving naturally between exploratory (breadth first) discussion and deeper analysis of single options (depth first) discussion.

- Too many interruptions can quickly derail even the best agenda.

- Too few interruptions probably indicates audience disengagement.

These problems all exist in physical meetings as well (as discussed in previous sections of the book) but they are exacerbated in the virtual because many of the human engagement cues needed to manage and engage the room are not present.

A further problem occurs with complex discussions that likely need several deep sessions of discussion. In a physical meeting, participants might be willing to dedicate two or three days for an offsite discussion on critical topics. This is much less palatable than three days of nonstop video conferences.

From all the various clients I've worked with, the biggest factors that affect the quality of a virtual team discussion are:

1. The size of the group. three to four people is often very effective and not much different from physical meetings. A group of 5–8 or even 10 is more challenging. More than 10 rarely works well and might be best restructured as a presentation followed by smaller discussions.

2. The skill of the moderator in ensuring that all participants

stay involved and sensing when people are approaching the need for a break in the proceedings.

3. A well-planned agenda that has long enough blocks for discussion but allows for meaningful breaks in which people can disengage. (The most effective pattern I've seen is discussion blocks of 75–90 minutes followed by 30–45-minute breaks.)

4. Ensuring that there is some kind of shared medium people can edit together or comment on, ideally something that will ultimately represent the output of the meeting. This may be a shared whiteboard, an online document, or the meeting chat stream.

We will deep dive into some more specific techniques in the following sections.

Virtual Watercoolers

One of the greatest losses of not having a physical office is that of the serendipitous conversation at the watercooler that can happen when colleagues bump into one another during short breaks. A more extreme version of this would be a work social event without a work agenda and people socializing instead.

In each case, the resulting conversations may be brief but can help make part of the information and social flow in an organization. An individual encounter may transfer an idea, connect some dots in an unusual but useful way, share news, or simply help refresh relationships.

In the virtual space, such meetings are harder to orchestrate because they don't occur naturally; however, some of the things that can be done instead include:

- Establishing a regular virtual (optional) social session. This "Happy Hour" in one large software team I worked with had between 10 and 15 people attending with a few announcements at the beginning but during the rest of the time people chatted about work and life-related topics. This worked well with about 10–15 people, but not so well with more.

- Randomized or non-work–related gatherings, e.g. virtual yoga, craft classes on line, or random chat with another team member during the week. In this case the formation of groups is driven by a common interest among team members that is not work related.

- Making sure there is time for personal exchange at the beginning of some or all team meetings. Keeping the first five or so minutes of online team meetings for general social chat and life/family updates may seem like a waste of time, but even a few minutes of such discussion gives people a quick insight into the lives of their colleagues and even their mood on that given day.

Spontaneous Meetings

These are a boon of the virtual world. The loss of a physical office often means there is less of an ability to just "drop in" on someone and ask a question. In reality, in a physical office, this still took time, and many companies have more than one location. Walking over to someone's desk is also a relatively immediate demand for attention. It is a synchronous request for a conversation, similar to a phone call.

In the virtual space a quick chat is arguably even easier and less intrusive. At one of the software startups I consult with there is an emerging culture of short one-to-one screen-sharing calls to resolve issues quickly. Anyone can ping a colleague with a chat message and ask for a quick conversation to clarify an issue or get help with something.

These interactions are often only 10–15 minutes long. When requested the other party does not have to say "yes" right away (as they might have felt pressured to if someone had walked to their desk). They can respond and say "sure, how about in an hour?"

or simply respond a little late if they are currently not checking messages.

These short meetings have a lower cost than meetings in the physical world and can provide a very useful layer of connection between team members that scheduled meetings do not.

IN PRACTICE

Understanding your context

- Try to classify each of your meetings into the types above. What type of meeting is each intended to be? What do they end up being when they are actually held? Are these the same thing?

- Assess whether some meeting types are needed but missing.

- Decide whether you have meeting types which are not listed here, and if so, think about whether they are effective or not.

Where are your biggest challenges?

- List which of the meeting types are working well and which are not.

- If you have many meetings which combine elements of different meeting types, assess whether the team would benefit from separating these out.

- For yourself personally, reflect on which of these meeting types feel most comfortable and which least comfortable. What would you like to improve most for yourself?

Virtual as an Individual

The first question in this new environment is: how should we act as individuals? In other words, what should we change about our communications behavior to be effective in this new world?

We'll start with listening, which becomes startlingly more difficult in virtual settings. Worse, if we know we are not listening well that probably means nobody else is either! Then we address the face—your own face. Next comes holding attention; finally, we finish with preparation.

Listening

Being in the same room with others in a meeting provides a powerful immediate anchor for attention. As humans we're wired to react to each other's physical presence and there are varying degrees of social norms about how distracted one can appear in the presence of others.

A close friend was once in Cuba for a conference at the national convention center when Fidel Castro was still in power. On the third day of the conference, attendees were hurriedly moved out of the conference space because "Fidel was coming." From the adjoining hotel they were then shown the television feed of Castro's resulting four-hour speech to a live audience in the conference center they had been in just hours before. The thing, however, that stuck with my friend was the 400–500 person audience who had appeared on demand and watched the speech. As the speech went on almost all of them began to move slightly in their chairs or exhibit occasional rocking motions. Many diligently, and with great effort, suppressed signs of tiredness or inattention. Clearly it did not pay to show anything other than rapt attention.

When sitting alone in a room during a virtual meeting, a participant does not have the physical presence of other people to hold their attention. It is also safer and much more tempting to multitask. The risk of being caught is much lower than face to face.

Worse still, virtual meetings stream video to your computer in a window on the desktop. This means that web browsers, email clients, and other distracting content are just a click away. It takes a great deal of willpower to ignore these temptations if the content of the meeting is not 100 percent on point.

Focusing on the meeting can be extremely difficult, but there are some strategies which can improve the situation:

- Minimize or shut down all other programs on your computer for important meetings. This is probably the single most important strategy for focus: Make the video calling app full screen. This can seem extreme and perhaps even wasteful; maybe you could check a few things while the meeting is going on? However, the other apps on the desktop can quickly pull more and more attention. Soon enough the meeting becomes an annoyance which is in the way of accomplishing small tasks like responding to an email. At that point, as a listener, you have already lost track of the meeting. If it were really true that it would be more productive to focus on the small tasks, perhaps it would be better not to attend the meeting or work to make the meeting more productive. On a video call it is also very often obvious when someone is working with other apps (it reflects in spectacles and/or their eyes dart between other stimuli). If minimizing other applications leads to the temptation to peek, then shutting down would be the better course. If certain applications are needed for the meeting itself, then clearly these should be an exception.

- Sit comfortably to listen. Each of us has sitting positions that are comfortable and uncomfortable. Each of us has sitting positions that enable and support good listening. We need several good listening sitting positions, so we can move back and forth between. Each of us has poor listening sitting positions. We need to know what they are so we can recognize when we slip into them.

- When a meeting is audio only, try walking. Try walking in different settings, at different paces, with different strides. Discover which settings, paces, and strides best enable your listening. Walking is beneficial, because it takes you away from distractions on your device screen and also relaxes you at the same time, making the audio content more present for you. Ideally, you can do this in a quiet environment, so if you do need to speak you can enable your microphone and do so. You may need to warn your colleagues ahead of time that you'll be doing this.

- You can also exercise in your chair. (If the meeting is a presentation, for example). With knees bent, lift your knee straight up and hold it. Straighten your leg and lift your whole leg off your chair. Place your elbows against the arms of the chair. With your back straight, lift your elbows up sideways, using the arms of the chair as resistance. These physical actions relax the body but leave you enough bandwidth to stay current with the conversation.

- Engage. Another way to focus is to ensure you interact with the meeting. An ideal start is to be the one to summarize. Push yourself to be part of the conversation as a summarizer. Ask clarifying questions. Ask substantive questions. Ask others what they think.

- Manage your breathing. When the exhale is longer than the inhale, the nervous system is calmed. When the inhale is longer than the exhale, the nervous system is excited. A calm nervous system leads to enhanced performance. An excited nervous system is prone to error.

The Face

While we may not be listening, we are often looking (and so are others). It is becoming the norm for meetings, especially those involving smaller groups, to have cameras active for most participants. This is generally great: it increases the connection between participants. It also, however, dramatically increases the importance of facial expressions in meeting settings.

In the virtual world, the face leads the way. It is front and center, in neon. We must get to know our face and its variety of faces (sad, mad, afraid, bored, interested, enticed, etc.) from the inside. We also must know what each of our faces communicates to others. When virtual, it helps to know, in the moment, what face we are wearing.

In a geographically dispersed, virtual organization, Raj, a project manager, wore a perpetual scowl during all meetings. Several times when I saw his scowl on the screen, I emailed him and said, "You look angry." He emailed right back and said he was not angry, but he was trying to listen as well as he could. Everyone he worked with got the impression that he was either angry or that Raj did not like them. No one liked working with him. He told me that his children were afraid of him. I suggested that he practice smiling in front of a mirror, that he work his way up to holding his smile in front of a mirror for 20 minutes. I suggested that he practice smiling in a mirror long enough that smiling becomes a habit.

In a one-on-one weekly meeting with me, his coach, he practiced holding a smile while discussing his difficult business issues. Whenever he dropped his smile, I said, "You dropped your smile." Then he would put his smile back on.

After several months of practice, Raj began catching himself scowling in meetings. When he caught himself, he dropped his scowl and put on his smile. Coworkers began noticing a difference in Raj. Some began to say they now liked working with him. Several more months later, Raj reported that his children no longer seemed afraid of him.

Getting comfortable with your face on the screen can be a major challenge. You can use these tips as preparation without having to be on an actual conference call:

1. Using a mirror or the screen of the device you use to videoconference, look at yourself.

2. Look at yourself until you can look without experiencing any emotional discomfort.

3. Recording yourself on a device, close your eyes and think of a situation in which you experience anger. Feel your way into the situation until it takes over your face.

4. Holding your angry face, feel which facial muscles are clenched. Clench them harder. Hold the clench.

5. Open your eyes. Pick one tight muscle at a time. On each exhale relax the muscle. Do this for each tight face muscle.

6. Sit in front of a mirror or screen, with your face perfectly relaxed.

7. Keeping your face relaxed, think of a virtual situation that causes you emotional discomfort. Keep your face relaxed while experiencing the emotional discomfort.

At first, doing these exercises seems like an exercise in vanity, and it can be deeply uncomfortable looking at one's own face in detail like this. Over time the practice gets easier for most people, however. It can be a shock to see how expressive your face can be, but it is a comfort to see that you do have some control over what it expresses!

Holding Attention

Given how difficult it is for each of us to listen in the virtual, it follows that for a presenter or meeting host it is equally challenging to hold the attention of an audience. Whether people can focus on the meeting, in fact, depends heavily on how the meeting is structured and run. We'll cover this meeting organizer role in later sections, but holding attention applies even if we are a speaker during only a segment of the meeting.

The challenge is different depending on the meeting type; but it applies most obviously to the presentation and group-discussion meetings.

One useful skill is recognizing distraction among the audience. You can do this even before you start speaking:

- Try to listen to any voices you hear—are they on topic or wandering to unrelated subjects?

- Are people's cameras on? Are they moving their eyes, heads, or hands? Are their heads darting on and off screen?

- Another common giveaway is if the participants are wearing spectacles; rapidly changing images on the screen often accidentally reflect as motion on those spectacles (sorry, spectacle wearers!).

None of this is to chastise those not paying attention; it is just to get a sense of the virtual room you are about to speak to.

Depending on how engaged the audience is you might want to try a combination of techniques to help hold their attention. The lifeblood of holding attention is dialogue over monologue. Turning what you say into dialogue versus monologue is the core of almost all attention-holding tools.

Depending on the meeting setting, engagement can work in two different ways:

1. In group discussion meetings: Turn your speaking into an opportunity to spark dialogue with others. Use techniques such as summarizing others before you speak, encouraging others to summarize you and ask questions, mentioning people's names when referring to their previous statements (to make your words an extension of theirs). Asking for a show of hands/votes in a chat is another way to engage the audience.

2. In presentations: Use words that create an inner dialogue in and with the participants. This means asking rhetorical questions, using statements that make the listener imagine

something ("Let's imagine we had no existing customer base to service, how would we approach the market? Think about that for a minute. What would it change?"), then follow up with your answers. Another tool for a longer presentation is to use other prepared speakers as part of the presentation. The listeners will immediately detect the change in speaker and focus on the dialogue.

At one of the software companies I worked with, Mike was leading the next major release. It was a very important release. The product had been losing market share and represented 50 percent of the company's revenues, as well as a little more than that in terms of profits. The team was stuck, falling behind schedule, and threatening the budget. Mike called a meeting, inviting the top two people in engineering, product marketing, marketing, and sales. Here is how he kicked off the meeting with this geographically dispersed team, spread over three continents.

"Ladies and gentlemen, it is heartwarming to see us all together, even if only virtually. It is important that we are all together because we have a very important problem to solve, which can only be solved if we solve it together.

"Please remember that I came out of a wonderful retirement to help you out and be able to work together, with you again. Right now, I am frustrated. What scares me is that I feel myself beginning to regret coming out of retirement.

"We are not working as a team. We are working as four teams each looking out for their own interests. Here is what I see. First let me say that after I share with you what I see, I want to hear from each of you, and hear what you see and think.

"It seems to me, when I compare product marketing's requirements with engineering's plan, it looks like engineering is discounting product marketing's requirements. When I read the email streams, it appears to me that product marketing is treating engineering with disrespect. After talking to a bunch of folks, it appears to me that marketing is not giving sales what it has asked for, while sales seems to be ignoring marketing's requests for sales data.

"So that is what I think I see. I am very interested in what the rest of you see. Before that, though, I wonder if someone might try to summarize what I just said."

Each time engineering spoke, Mike made sure that someone in product marketing summarized, and vice versa. When someone from sales spoke, Mike made sure that someone from marketing summarized, and vice versa. People were saying things they had thought about for some time but were saying for only the first time. They raised issues that needed to be managed better yet had not been openly discussed before.

The meeting was still extremely challenging and arguably would have been easier if everyone was physically in the same place. However, with his candor up front and calls for summaries, Mike made sure everyone paid attention and engaged in the meeting.

Preparation

For an individual attending a meeting, it is tempting to think of the meeting as something that happens in a bounded period of time and stands alone. However, we can be much more productive if we see the meeting as existing in a workflow or decision making or some other flow.

One of the small tricks mentioned earlier in the book for weekly team sync meetings is to have an open agenda document that anybody can add topics to. This has worked well at several organizations I've worked with. The reason it works is twofold. First, it cuts the period of time at the start of the meeting needed to negotiate what will be discussed. Second, it means that participants can glance at the list ahead of time and organize their thoughts for the discussions which are important to them.

Looking at the agenda and any materials ahead of time, even for just 10 minutes, is very valuable: it allows you as a participant to identify what the key parts of the meeting will be for you. Ironically, the provided materials for a meeting can be a distraction to many participants if they are not read ahead of time. The temptation is to try to read them during the beginning of the meeting in real time while simultaneously trying to listen to the meeting facilitator. This is why meetings at Amazon under Jeff Bezos famously included a reading period at the beginning of meetings ["How Jeff Bezos Has Run Amazon, From Meetings to Managing" By Lauren Weber, *Wall Street Journal*, Feb. 2 ,2021].[1]

If you are the host, you can take a number of other steps that hugely improve the effectiveness of meetings:

- Share materials up front as much as you can. This not only helps the participants; it also increases your own preparedness and comfort in the meeting.

- If there are multiple speakers in the meeting, try to establish the practice that all speakers share materials beforehand. This is also a way to ensure the protagonists in the meeting are themselves prepared.

- If appropriate, open a shared document ahead of time in which people can add topics, questions, or observations they would like addressed in the meeting.

- Have questions ready for the audience; ideally, tell presenters what the questions are at the beginning so they know these will be coming at the end.

Ted, a lab manager, had completed a yearlong training program I led. He asked me to do an analysis of his leadership. His team was virtual, spread over four continents. I interviewed his top eight people virtually. Most complained about Ted's temper and his constant changing of direction. A meeting was scheduled for me to give Ted feedback with his top eight reports participating—or so I had assumed.

---

[1] Lauren Weber, "How Jeff Bezos Has Run Amazon, From Meetings to Managing," *Wall Street Journal*, Feb. 2, 2021.

When the meeting began, only one of the eight faces on the screen belonged to someone I had interviewed. The one present was the only one who did not complain about Ted's anger and constant changing of direction. When I presented each item of criticism, Ted asked, "Does anyone agree with this?" No one attending the meeting agreed.

It became clear to me that I had made two mistakes. First, during the training program Ted had never shown himself open to criticism and I had ignored this fact. It was the beginning of my career, and I ignored the obvious signs that this was a set-up for failure. My second error was my failure to be explicit with Ted about who should attend the feedback meeting. In fact, I had said to him, "Invite who you like," assuming it would be obvious that his top eight reports would be on that list.

On the first point I should have thought through how the meeting might play out, given Ted's attitude. This should have led me to be up front with Ted about his lack of engagement with feedback and to try to get him to be more open to it. On the second point I should have been a lot more careful about who would be at the meeting and how the order of speaking would go. A lot more work should have gone into making it a safe environment for people to voice their concerns.

Unfortunately, once a meeting is off track like this it is very hard to recover both the meeting and the process of change you may be trying to enact. In preparation it is really important to focus on the outcome you are aiming at and work through how you expect each of the participants to act.

It was the late 1980s. A major credit card company was in the midst of a major overhaul of their IT system. I got a call from a friend and colleague at Wharton. He had a client who had a difficult political minefield to navigate. Would I be interested in helping his client? I love this kind of problem. I asked my friend to tell me about his client. What kind of difficult feedback does he receive, and what does he do with it? He told me a couple of stories, and I said I would very much like to talk to his client, Tom. Tom was a senior vice president, in charge of the IT overhaul.

We talked. Tom was in Kansas City, headquarters of engineering. Everybody else was in New York, as were all the C-level executives, finance, marketing, sales. There was a deep and bitter disagreement between engineering and marketing. There had been a significant and sudden decline of transactions cleared through the company's clearinghouse. Engineering, which ran the clearinghouse, insisted this was a one-time aberration. Marketing declared this was the first tremors of an avalanche, in which banks would bypass the clearinghouse to clear transactions directly among themselves.

These two competing visions required radically different IT overhauls. The project team had gone as far as it could without a decision on which vision to build. A decision was needed. Tom requested a meeting of the C team. We had three weeks to prepare. Tom and I prepared by phone. The first time Tom and I met was the night before the meeting in Manhattan.

Tom led the meeting. Throughout the meeting, he invited summary and inquiry. He articulated both visions. He described the significant differences between systems requirements for both visions. He said that the project had gone as far as it could go. A decision was needed. The project could not proceed without one.

Near the end of the meeting a McKinsey consultant came up to me and said that he had never seen anyone so well prepared for a difficult meeting. He was amazed when I told him it had all been done by phone.

At the end of the meeting the CEO said it was one of the best presentations he had ever witnessed. This was followed by standing applause. A decision was made two weeks later.

All meetings (physical and virtual) require preparation, so this outcome isn't unique to a virtual scenario. However, in the previous case, Ted would have been much less likely to call a physical feedback meeting without his key direct reports. The virtual environment made the meeting seem a little less critical and allowed Ted to sidestep some of the consequences.

IN PRACTICE

- For the key meetings you have coming up, if you are the organizer: decide carefully what type of meeting you are aiming for and distinguish carefully between segments of presentation, discussion, and other types.

- For presentations, plan out interactive elements in the flow (questions, answers, cameos from other speakers) to get the right level of interactivity. Also make a plan for getting the audience to ask questions.

- Again, if you are the meeting facilitator and especially if you are the main speaker, ask others to summarize; make this a regular practice.

- Ensure the meeting agenda is shared with attendees before the meeting and summarized at the meeting start. Tell people if there are questions/discussions at the end—what are they going to be?

- Make sure everybody at the meeting actually needs to be there. As in the case with Ted's feedback you may also need to ensure certain people who need to be there will definitely be at the meeting.

- Try to have at least five-minute gaps between meetings so you can gather yourself.

- Craft the messages you want to communicate and the questions you want to ask beforehand.

VIRTUAL AS A TEAM

No matter how much we do as individuals, the outcomes of meetings depend heavily on all the participants involved (even those desperately trying to finish a client email while the meeting is running).

In this section we'll talk about team dynamics in the virtual world, starting with agendas before covering interruptions and what to do for especially long meetings.

Agenda Setting

There is a set of common errors that hinder the management of meeting agendas, and these often have even more negative effects in a virtual setting. Because virtual meetings are often treated as somewhat less important or costly than physical meetings, agenda creation is sometimes skipped entirely or only done in a cursory fashion.

Absence of an agenda

Meetings that lack an agenda waste far too much time. In some organizations people rail against this and the practice stops, but in others it is tolerated as "just the way it is."

Thirty years ago, the director of a well-known high-tech research center asked me to sit in on a staff call. The staff spent the first half hour of an hour-long meeting deciding what they should talk about first. I interrupted at the half hour mark. I asked if this was an atypical meeting. They assured me all their meetings went like this. I suggested they address the first question that comes into the director's head. Once the staff engaged the question, I prompted summarizing. At the end of the meeting, those who spoke agreed that the conversation was as good as they had had, which I was shocked to hear. Some meetings ended up with a long list of topics, others were of little import with everyone distracted.

This level of dysfunction is somewhat of an outlier, but in many teams I have worked with it is common practice to have meetings that start with no set topics other than some standard reporting items. This occurs not only for staff meetings, but also for group discussions where a high-level topic is set but no agenda is set on how the discussion should proceed.

For the research team, I asked that the team members each come to their next staff meeting with ideas on what an agenda management process could look like as well as topics prepared. Their staff meetings were significantly improved by creating a virtual "call for topics" document which anyone could add items to up until the beginning of the meeting and by appointing a coordinator for the meeting who would lead prioritizing the items in the first five minutes of the call. This used the virtual nature of the meeting well: giving everyone access to a shared document of agenda items they could all contribute to on screen right up until meeting start and then forming the shared agenda. Their meetings became much more satisfying, covering many more issues than previously.

For group discussions with an overall topic (often an important decision to be made) it may seem that "discuss X" is enough of an agenda. However, if a decision is to be successful it is critical to identify how the decision itself will be made and confirmed (by voting? By one decision maker?) and what contributions are needed before this happens. The two most common ways such meetings go off the rails are:

- Lack of preparation from someone expected to shed a light on some aspect of the decision. "We need to know last quarter's marketing numbers to make this decision, do you have them Ted?"

- Members of the group feeling that not all voices have been heard before the final decision is due and arguing for more time.

The first of these can be mitigated a great deal by having an agenda that makes clear who should speak on which topic so they can prepare. The second may sometimes be the right call: when a decision needs more work, then it needs to get the attention it deserves. Often however, when it is clear on the agenda that a decision must be made and by what method, parties in the room focus on the most critical elements of the topic earlier so they can complete the task.

Absence of Social Time

Social time humanizes meetings and invites empathy so that we can more deeply feel fellow participants as human beings. It lessens the difficulty of difficult conversations and decisions. Empathy enhances the chances of successfully having productive results from difficult conversations. The absence of social time does not invite empathy. The strain of difficult conversations and decisions is not lessened. The degree of difficulty remains high.

From interviews with team members in one company, it appeared to me that the team was very businesslike, did not like to waste time, and did not waste time. They prided themselves on the efficiency of their meetings. They always got through their agenda items and always started and ended on time. Yet something was missing from the interviews.

On teams with high morale, during interviews, when asked, "What is working well?" interviewees are effusive about what the team and individuals are doing and how they are doing it. Admiration, affection, and respect are expressed. No one on this team was effusive when asked what was done well. Before staff meetings there was no social interaction. Everyone linked in on time, just before the meeting. No one said anything until the team's leader formally started the meeting. In their staff meetings there was no humor, no playfulness. It was not clear to me that the teammates liked each other.

Despite their lack of spirit, their productivity and profitability were good. I thought that if they could relate to each other as human beings and develop empathy they could perform even better, with less effort. I said this to them. They thought my idea was worth a try. I suggested that they start the meeting 10 minutes earlier or end it 10 minutes later. I suggested that each week, each member share something they think their teammates do not know about them. Each week, one team member had to bring something funny to read to the team. When the experiment was six weeks old, there was some humor and playfulness at every meeting. They decided to extend the experimental period to a quarter of an hour. Privately, team members said that they now enjoyed team meetings. Some said that now was the first time they felt like they were on a team.

A year later, profits had improved more than expected, and productivity also improved more than expected. Every member of the team said that getting to know each other explained the improvements.

I have since advocated a similar pattern with almost all the teams I work with. The benefits go much deeper than purely monetary results. The increased empathy between team members sparks new ideas and, also, a greater sense of well-being in the team. This in turn encourages team members to think of the team first, creating a cycle of increasing team togetherness.

Too Many Agenda Items

When an agenda has too many items, at least a few, if not all, will not get the discussion required to produce a satisfactory result. This is a common error. Too many agenda setters produce another common error: they confuse the best case for the most likely case, underestimating the time each agenda item requires.

Example: Every member of the team was frustrated with his or her meetings. No item was ever discussed to a satisfactory resolution. Every team member was able to put items on the agenda. There was no gatekeeper. Each meeting began with a negotiation over how much time would be allotted to each item. This negotiation took a quarter of the meeting time.

When it was suggested that a gatekeeper might help with managing the agenda, members objected, saying that was not democratic.

An Important Item Is Not on the Agenda

It is surprising how often this happens. A key issue, requiring almost immediate discussion, does not make the agenda. There are several ways this happens. The agenda setter is unaware that an issue needs urgent discussion; sometimes, no one wants to face an issue and it is treated as taboo; other times, someone does not raise an issue for fear it will harm his or her place in the group.

Example: All but one member of the leadership team expressed serious concern about the absence of an engineering plan two quarters before the product launch was scheduled. The item never made the agenda because the CEO refused to put it on, concerned that doing so would seriously harm the head of engineering.

The Wrong People Control the Agenda

Usually, when the wrong person sets the agenda, the wrong things are discussed at the meeting. Who is the right person to set the agenda? It does not have to be the team's leader. It should be someone who has a well-informed overview of the team's goals, objectives, and operations, and of the current situation of all elements the team is responsible for. The agenda manager should be trusted and respected by members of the team.

In a Los Angeles city councilman's office, a key Friday afternoon meeting never addressed the issues the meeting was intended to address. The press secretary's secretary, who was unaware of what the meeting was meant to address, managed the agenda. The meeting became productive once the chief of staff took over managing the agenda.

Interruptions

There are productive interruptions and unproductive interruptions. Productive interruptions enable the following actions: to summarize what has been presented, to ask a clarifying or substantive question, or to interrupt someone who is changing the subject, headed down a rabbit hole, or derailing the conversation. When a presentation offering complex information goes on for more than a paragraph or two, an interruption to summarize is often wise. Unproductive interruptions lead to changing the subject, going down rabbit holes, derailing discussion.

There are individuals, and groups, that have the habit of interrupting. When this is the case, almost all the interrupting is unproductive. With some individuals, pointing out interruptions helps them reduce their interrupting. Others get defensive and persist.

The best virtual teams that I know have a lively use of productive interruptions, while producing few, if any, unproductive interruptions.

I led a study group consisting of 10 senior independent management consultants in Silicon Valley for four years. Two years after the group started, a new member, Jeff, joined. Jeff was very successful at designing and leading training programs. He was also a brilliant diagnostician of complex organizational issues. However, he estimated that he had been fired from at least half of the organizational development projects he led.

In the first two hours of the first meeting of the study group that Jeff attended, he interrupted others four times. Each time he changed the subject. At the end of each discussion, we discussed the discussion. It was time to give Jeff feedback. I waited. No one seemed willing to start so I did. I said to Jeff, "During the discussion of Alice's case, you interrupted four times and changed the subject each time."

Jeff responded by asking the group, "Did I really interrupt

four times?" Members of the group assured him that he had. Jeff expressed surprised. He was unaware of interrupting. Over the next four hours Jeff interrupted another six or seven times. Just before the meeting ended, Alice, another member, asked Jeff, "Is this how you behave when you are consulting?" Jeff said he did not know, but he imagined so. Alice suggested that he bring two audio tapes to our next meeting, one, she suggested, of his consulting, and one of his training.

After listening to the two tapes at the next meeting, George said to Jeff, "In the training tape, you listened and inquired. In the consulting tape, you interrupted and advocated. If I had a consultant who interrupted constantly, I would fire him, too."

Jeff asked the group's help in learning to avoid interrupting. He asked us to interrupt his interruptions. We did. By Jeff's sixth meeting he did not interrupt once. He was never fired from another consulting job again.

In virtual meetings interruptions can be the only indicator that the meeting is dynamic, lively, and has engaged participants. It can be productive to interrupt when the speaker seems to have been speaking too long without a break. On the other hand, as we already learned earlier, interruptions can be terribly disruptive to a meeting's progress.

Over time, in many teams I've tended to classify the level of interruptions in a discussion into three states:

1. The speaker speaks, but there are no interruptions
2. The speaker speaks and people interrupt but disrupt and derail.
3. The speaker speaks and there are interactions that indicate interest, add to the conversation, but do not derail.

The first state could be because this is a presentation meeting, and all is well: listeners are focused on the content and following good etiquette in not interrupting. In most cases, however, in a virtual meeting this is a bad sign because the other explanation is that no-one is paying attention.

The third state shows genuine engagement and a great discussion in progress.

The second state would definitely be considered bad in most meetings, but in virtual meetings it is most likely a better situation that being in the first state where no one is paying attention. An engaged audience can be managed and encouraged to use better protocols for interaction. A non-engaged audience is generally a sign of deeper problems.

Long meetings

Deep topics require long meetings; sometimes multiple hours but sometimes multiple days of discussion are required. In physical meetings, long discussions are broken up naturally by meal breaks, coffee, walks, and interactions in the hallway. The thought of virtual meetings of a similar length brings on a sense of dread. It hardly seems feasible that a team could spend three days, all day, in video calls without suffering breakdowns. Nevertheless, those thorny topics still need to be discussed—so how can it be done?

The first step is to determine whether the long meeting is really needed or whether there are other ways to resolve the discussions at hand. These might include:

- Using a shared document to allow anyone in the group to propose solutions to the problems at hand.
- Identifying a small group (or more than one) to draw up a concrete set of proposals for the choice to be made to boil down the options.
- Getting initial feedback on proposed decisions using a voting or scoring system to get an idea of where sentiment lies.

All of these can reduce the amount of time needed in a synchronous meeting. However, sometimes even these items will not reduce the amount of time needed enough. On complex emotive topics and on those where quick back-and-forth iterations are needed, there is little substitute for interacting synchronously in a meeting.

Once it is clear that a long stretch of time is really needed, it is important to try to accommodate the normal rhythms and breaks that would accompany a similar physical meeting and that don't create too much discomfort. Time block strategies that have been effective for some of the teams I have worked with include:

- 90 mins on, 30 mins off for two or three cycles

- Three blocks of 90 mins for two or three days, scheduling the blocks mostly in the morning so that afternoons are free (or vice versa) depending on the time zone of each participant).

- A full day with flexible starting and stopping for each topic, but with a predefined long lunch slot of 90–120 minutes.

Each team is likely to have a unique perfect division of meeting time to break time. When the topic is important and complex, and the dialogue is vibrant, and the communication tools are applied, three hours can fly by. However, this is rarely the case even for a single block of meeting time. I find that, for me, old man that I am, more than two hours is hard to do, and 90 minutes as a maximum time block seems to work even better. An hour tends to be too little time to really deep dive into a topic.

The content and agenda of the meeting are also extremely important. Given that the team has decided to make the investment in having such a long meeting, one can assume that the topic is indeed important. All the challenges of a normal meeting still apply, though: the need to have clear objectives for the meeting, the need for the content to be engaging, the need to ensure that all voices are heard.

Some suggestions to help ensure the right outcomes include:

- Determine which time blocks are for presentation and which for discussion.

- Share as much of the material as possible up front and encourage groups to prepare content ahead of time, including using voting or feedback tools to get a sense of sentiment on a topic before the discussion starts.

- Make sure there is adequate social time during the meeting, whether this is in each time block, during breaks, or as its own scheduled item.

As the meeting progresses, it is important to check regularly on whether progress is being made toward its objectives and on how engaged the participants are feeling. Asking everyone regularly how they feel helps in this regard. Changing the length of some sessions or moving breaks can be very helpful if morale is sagging.

IN PRACTICE

1. For your next long meeting, identify what kind of meeting each session should ideally be and make sure the objectives of the meeting are clearly understood by everybody.

2. Think back to previous meetings and assess what role interruptions played. Identify the positive and negative interruptions and see if there are any patterns you could make the meeting groups aware of.

3. In meetings when participants begin struggling with their listening, it is time to break, so try suggesting one. This is easy if you are the organizer, but you can do it even if you aren't. Your colleagues will likely thank you if you instigate everyone getting a break.

VIRTUAL COMMUNICATIONS CULTURE

Communications culture tends to fit one of two extremes: meetings are not treated with much respect and tend to meander and feel like a waste of time; or they are treated as sacred times in which high expectations are set for all participants. Many teams even oscillate between these two states over time, with a descent into poor meeting discipline followed by a willful attempt to achieve meeting purity.

In reality neither extreme is realistic or desirable. What is important is to establish a functioning, respectful communications culture that delivers the results that the organization needs. Within this framework there will always be some people who have to multitask a little on a given day or some meetings which don't go well. The key in these cases is to have a functioning and open dialogue about the meeting culture itself—on what to improve and what is/is not acceptable.

General communications culture is covered in Part III of the book; however, some items of culture are specific to virtual environments. We start with the use of cameras.

Cameras at the Ready

As virtual meetings took off during the COVID-19 pandemic, the use of cameras during video conferencing also rose significantly. Some teams left it open to every attendee whether to use a camera during a call; others stated that people were generally expected to do so. As people grew accustomed to being in meetings from their own personal spaces and, sometimes, at unusual hours, the use of cameras could feel like an invasion of privacy at times, a new source of stress. A video camera interaction can in some ways feel more intimate than a one-on-one meeting, because it has much more emphasis on the face than the rest of the body.

It's simplistic to say that cameras are good or bad for meetings. Their benefits and challenges are highly dependent on the situation.

However, teams with more camera use do tend to feel closer, in my experience.

A good friend who worked at one of the software companies I consulted for was very used to virtual meetings because the company had mixed remote and office work since the early 2000s. She was regularly on calls with colleagues around the globe. Moving to a smaller startup in early 2020 after the pandemic hit, she found a culture that prioritized having cameras on during calls unless there was some particular reason (such as being in transit or having some local challenge). After experiencing this for some time she came to the realization that she highly valued seeing other faces and turned her own camera on almost all the time. This value hadn't been a priority at the larger global organizations and many people regularly did not connect their cameras on calls.

The difference in understanding for others on the team was significant. The smaller startup environment did help but even at the larger company many of the teams she had worked with had been small.

This is a common experience across multiple teams I have worked with: the humanizing effect of seeing other faces seems to go deep.

Cameras can also make us more aware of our own persona in a meeting. A client law firm went virtual during the pandemic. At his very first virtual meeting, a senior litigator was shocked to see his own face on his monitor. He asked to have the meeting recorded. It was. At the end of this first meeting he said, "I was shocked to see how fierce I look. Do I look fierce to you all? And do I look like this all the time?"

He was assured that he did look fierce, and that he always looked that way. He then asked to have every meeting he participated in recorded. He looked at himself in each meeting to see how fierce he looked. Within a month he had taught himself to look bemused and interested. His closest associates told him how much easier it was to be in meetings with him.

All in all there is no "right" policy on camera use, but defaulting to more cameras definitely seems to lead to a more engaged and empathetic team experience.

Sidebar Communications

One of the features of virtual meetings that is generally not present in physical meetings is the ability to "chat" virtually with other meeting participants while in the meeting itself. In some meeting cultures meeting chats get little use, but in others they are alive with commentary and additional information.

For presentations, some meeting platforms provide not only a participant chat feature but also dedicated Q&A channels. In these channels questions can be asked and then answered by a team working with the speaker in real time or by the speaker after their presentation has ended.

In general, having an active chat during a session (both presentations and discussion meetings) shows positive engagement from the audience. The chat messages show people are paying attention and engaged with the topic. The traffic on the side channel can get out of hand, however.

In one large software company I worked with, a companywide presentation was organized to announce the news that the company was going to be acquired by an even larger firm. This was mixed news for many employees and, given the nature of this announcement, there were many unknowns for employees on acquisition day. During the presentation of the acquisition details and the subsequent Q&A, the chat exploded with commentary. Some of the commentary was positive, other items raised important questions, but a significant proportion was highly negative and critical, to the extent that some posters may have regretted their posts later on.

On the positive side, this gave the senior team a real-time insight into sentiment; it also quickly surfaced key questions to answer. On the negative side some of the comment threads were harsh and, in some cases, ill-advised. To some extent, also, the comment thread drew more attention than the message the speakers were trying to get across.

As with camera usage, there is no easy answer to whether sidebar communications should be encouraged. However, in general they add a positive dynamic of engagement. A few considerations include:

- Are people staying on topic in the chat or wandering off topic? If the latter, it will be useful to give guidance not to do this.

- Side-channel discussions between individuals may happen anyway and may be distracting. Providing a common forum for side-chat may be beneficial in that it brings the conversation to everybody.

- If conversations are on topic but increasing in volume, with the speaker unaware of the messages, this can be a distraction. It can be useful to have a moderator either indicate to the speaker that they may want to address an issue in the chat, or to post in the chat to let people know the speaker will address an issue later.

- Another useful application of the sidebar chat is as the place where people can raise a hand to speak. Some virtual meeting platforms have this feature built in, but if not, establishing a simple protocol (type "raise hand" in the chat) can be very effective. This is a way of facilitating interruptions and introducing new points without being disruptive to whomever is speaking.

Having a focal point and collaborative editing

Another feature of meetings which is more powerful in the virtual than it is in a physical meeting is collaborative editing. Shared documents, virtual whiteboards, or pair-programming tools allow more than one person (and often everyone) to productively edit something everyone can see.

In a physical meeting this can still occur with a shared document projected up on a screen with everyone looking at their own screen in a replication of what we could do in virtual. More often in a physical meeting, though, the "shared" media might be a flip chart or blackboard which people walk to in order to write. These can have their own positive dynamic, a physicality and the sense of something real being built; but they can also often lead to one person dominating the conversation.

In one of the small software teams I work with, their regular virtual ideation meetings use a Miro whiteboard very productively. The meetings move between times when individuals (or pairs) can chew on a problem and drop their ideas onto the whiteboard as sticky notes, mind maps, or other constructs, and a group discussion where each individual talks through what they added. The team then draws out the elements from each contribution into one larger construct that either summarizes the common points (an intersection of the ideas) or pulls in all the unique items (a union of ideas). The use of the whiteboard engages everyone in the discussion.

Live editing a text document can also work for this: allowing each participant to express their thoughts in text and then aggregating the result. For things such as agendas this works extremely well. For complex texts it tends to work better if, after each participant has presented their text and highlighted key points, the key focus of the text is agreed upon and a smaller group does the final editing.

Not every meeting benefits from collaborative editing in this manner, but certain group discussions in particular can use it very effectively. It is one case where being 100 percent virtual may be genuinely better than in person.

Don't Accidentally Devalue the Virtual

Respecting the other participants in a meeting, whether it be the other party in a one-on-one or people one barely knows in a large meeting, is key to communication in any context. This seems obviously true for both virtual and physical meetings. Unfortunately, it can be easy to treat virtual meetings as just by their nature somehow "less important" or "more informal".

This "devaluing" can sometimes be benefit. It can remove the tension from a one-on-one, and it can help someone nervous about a meeting prepare and not worry about body language as much (though remember that your face is much more in view).

In many cases, though, there is a danger that the devaluing of the meeting leads to sloppiness: not showing up to the call on time, not having audio/video and so forth prepared, being in a space where one has to interact with others outside the meeting, or dressing down even when the topic is important.

Each of these behaviors can signal to the other parties that the meeting is not that important. Which in turn can signal a lack of respect for the topic and the other participants. Meetings that start off on the wrong foot like this risk not generating the right outcome or, possibly worse, eroding long-term trust among the participants.

Another very important way in which respect plays into virtual meetings is the recognition of the participants involved. For a physical meeting there is a "meet and greet" phase as people walk into the room, acknowledge one another, and exchange a word or two. In virtual meetings this is often skipped. For outgoing, talkative participants this probably doesn't matter too much because they will almost certainly feel "heard" before the meeting is over. For more introverted individuals, however, it can lead to meetings that feel as though no-one knows they are there at all.

One geographically dispersed organization I worked with had people spread from the American northwest, to Australia, New Zealand, north Africa, London, Manchester, and Copenhagen.

Maddie, the leader, always expressed her care and concern for whomever she met with. The same was true of every member of her leadership team. Each was an excellent and eager listener. Every meeting began with a check-in with each participant. The response to participants' check-ins ranged from laughter and applause to tears and virtual hugs. Every participant in every meeting was given the appropriate time and space to speak. This does take time, but it's a great investment for team morale and inclusiveness.

Following up

Sensing how people are reacting to discussion and decisions is a key part of really listening. In physical meetings this happens in real time and as you improve your listening there are often moments where you realize one or another person may not have reacted in the way you expected. Perhaps they were unhappy with a decision and chose not to share that fact; perhaps they were particularly enthusiastic about something but no-one else in the room realized it.

In a physical meeting there are often moments as you file out of the meeting room and head off to other parts of the building where you can catch up with someone and mention your perception. Saying things like "You seemed unhappy with that outcome, what could have been done better?" or "When we talked about the upcoming conference you seemed very enthusiastic but perhaps the organizer didn't realize that," and so on might help you understand a situation better and capture opportunities to improve that are currently being missed.

In a virtual meeting the moods and reactions of people are much harder to gauge (especially if cameras are off) and these moments leaving a meeting don't really happen. The call ends and everyone is instantly disconnected.

I've seen two practices that bring in a culture of following up to a team after big decisions:

- The first is to try to ask all meeting attendees their feelings after a decision has been taken. They are invited to share right there and then if they have any issues with the outcome.

- The second is that those leading the team make sure they follow up with, ideally, all key team members, but at least those most affected by a decision. The follow-up can be as lightweight as a direct message chat or as complete as a follow-up one-on-one chat.

The purpose of these discussions isn't to undo or question a decision but to understand how team members feel about the choice. This helps managers mitigate negative impacts, it helps spot opportunity, and above all it communicates to the team members that they are valued.

A Touch of the Real

This section of the book is about virtual communication. While it's certainly possible to operate fully virtually all of the time, and several of my clients do, realistically most of the best virtual teams I know still meet face to face regularly, at least once a quarter.

These regular meetings serve as an anchor point for many of the relationships in the team that can then be built upon in the virtual.

A customer service organization I worked with met once a quarter for three days. Their time together combined important, difficult discussion with great fun and good food. Another of my favorite virtual teams, an e-game company building its first game, met for two weeks once a quarter. They, too, combined difficult discussion, great fun, and good food. My hunch is that the customer service organization needed less time together because the collaboration required was simple, with minimal communicated detail. For the e-gamers collaboration required highly detailed and complex collaboration; they needed very deep, complex common understanding and agreement on what would be done next by whom, by when? It took the two weeks to discuss everything that needed discussing.

As work normalizes again and the world becomes more accustomed to living with COVID-19, many organizations are looking at their work practices. The best organizations are trying to combine what worked well in virtual with what worked well in in-person meetings.

This sounds good in theory, but for many organizations there is also a cost element to going back to the office and having in-person meetings. Especially for those with globally distributed teams, travel budgets were cut to zero during the pandemic and it is tempting to keep them as low as possible, despite travel opportunities opening up again. Some of this is warranted: potentially there are meetings which did not need to happen in person, and many people are not yet ready to travel as much as before since health risks still exist.

Being too restrictive on travel budget constraints is likely a mistake, however; it is certainly true that much more can now be done virtually than before, but teams still benefit hugely from getting together in person. Investing in spaces to regularly have those meetings and in travel to facilitate team meeting is still a very worthwhile investment to make even while continuing many of the virtual practices.

In Practice

1. Consider whether there is an explicit virtual communications culture at your organization.
2. If there is, is it followed? Or is behavior rather different?
3. Are there elements of the culture which you believe could be improved or at least made more explicit?
4. To refine the culture, it helps greatly if the leader is an exemplar of excellent listening and particularly of respect. Who are the leaders shaping communications culture? Are they aware that they are doing so, or do they need a nudge?

PART VI

MASTERY: A ROAD PAVED WITH GLASS AND GOLD

Mastery is comprehensive knowledge or skill at something. It is the ability to do things in a given domain that might have seemed impossible when starting out. Yet it is a journey rather than a destination: levels of comprehension and skill unlock new possibilities that themselves reveal new levels of mastery not yet reached or imagined.

Mastery is taking right action without thinking. There is something very delicious about taking right action without thinking. There is no doubt, no hesitation, no fear. There is no self. There is a lightness, an ease. At first it is a relief, and then it becomes delicious.

There are levels of mastery. Some say the first level is achieved after 10,000 hours of practice. We practice until each action is embedded deeply in our bodies. Once actions are deeply embedded in our bodies, we can act without thinking. Action then bypasses the mind. Action becomes instinctive. If we have practiced with discipline and reflection, the action embedded is right action. When we practice without discipline, we are at risk of embedding bad habits, which is where we began, with the bad habits of defensiveness.

Communication in our daily lives is something many of us take for granted. We learn to converse, to write, to send emails and how to join a video meeting, but we assume the way people communicate "is what it is." Yet, as we've seen in the previous parts of this book, almost every aspect of communication could be improved to make us and those around us happier. Mastery of interpersonal communication is a wonderful investment, even if it can be painful at times.

As we become more aware of our own defensiveness and how others react, we start to know what to do without thinking, even in complex situations. As we get better at communicating in many situations there is less emphasis on self, less self-consciousness, and less concern about how others think of us. Our being and body are present and at one, in the moment, knowing what to do without thinking.

Mastery of the interpersonal realm requires alertness to situations that might prompt or trigger defensiveness. This requires awareness of ourselves, others, and groups, and of situations where defensiveness is being triggered. Increasingly competent use of the tools and processes deepens awareness of the presence of the intangibles within a team.

The levels of mastery in the interpersonal realm are inexhaustible. There are always new questions, new curiosities, new skills, and deeper, more nuanced knowledge to master. Mastery is practicing all the time. Practice incrementally deepens and broadens our awareness, with increasing nuance. Our experience is constantly in discovery, seeking facts and insights, learning, increasing competence, and in delightful surprise. It is being in the moment fully, knowing what to do without thinking, bypassing the mind, feeling the flow.

These moments, when they occur, feel like breakthroughs in understanding. In the next moment however, one can again feel like a beginner at the task.

My own experience of cultivating mastery, and my experience supporting clients in cultivating their mastery, reveal a sequence of iterative steps during the ongoing journey; we discover variance between our intentions and our actions. The discovery is accompanied by unwanted emotions. It takes time and reflection to accept one's unwanted behavior. Once we accept that the variance is real and true, we commit, to ourselves, to correct the variance. We practice. We seek feedback on our practice. We keep practicing.

This feels like a continuous journey of improvement.

There is continual practice and intermittent progress. Then, one day, weeks, or months, or years later, we discover that we are using our new tool without thinking about it. It has become instinctive.

In this part of the book, we will cover practices which can help deepen our understanding and competence in communication. It begins with beginner's mind.

BEGINNER'S MIND IN COMMUNICATION

The notion of "beginner's mind" is somewhat hard to grasp. My own understanding of beginner's mind is that the beginning of anything is uncomfortable, filled with impatience with myself for not being better, for not knowing. As soon as I start practicing a new tool or yoga practice, I am impatient with myself. I hurry through the practice, barely aware of what I am doing, uncomfortable with my not knowing how to do it better. Then I remember that I have gone through this many times. I know how to learn. I need to slow down, stick with it, and persevere. At some unknown time in the future, I will discover that I am using the tool or doing the practice without thinking about it.

The Buddhist version of beginner's mind is being open to learning. It includes the attitude that there is always more to learn that will bring delight, surprise, and utility. I embrace the Buddhist version, and have found it true, over and over again, and not just for me but for clients, friends, and family.

At the beginning of learning a new tool, focus is essential. In the context of mastering the tools, focus is reminding ourselves constantly, all day, to remain in the moment and apply the tool you are learning. Discipline is required to practice consistently and enough. Feedback from others is needed to assess how well you are practicing the new tool.

Learning and applying the tools, processes, and intangibles in this handbook can seem like a daunting task. It is a career-long and, perhaps, lifelong journey. There are many things to remember, and some of the suggested practices— such as raising important taboo issues—can be highly uncomfortable. Many of the suggestions are also very difficult to apply: being aware of one's own feelings when speaking, catching oneself when one isn't really listening, and so forth. These all take practice.

The good news is that everyone is in the same boat, but you have already taken a necessary step in being curious about how communication could be better.

Beginner's mind can be hugely helpful in exploring how to make things better:

- There is no need to practice every technique at once. Choose a few of the ones which you feel could make an immediate impact for you and focus on those. See what they teach you.

- Each day at work or with family is a new experience. How are people in the room reacting to your boss's monologues? How do people react when you give them a summary of what they just said before making your own point?

- There is no shame in making a mistake or recognizing a negative behavior. I grew proud of owning my mistakes and exploring them in depth and critically. No one expects an athlete to run an Olympic record time on their first outing. There are many steps along the way.

- Even those who have paid attention to their communication for many years make mistakes and get frustrated; they experience new revelations just as often as someone just starting out.

In these ways, beginner's mind helps us see that we are always on a journey of improvement and that there are interesting things to see along the way.

However, there is a trap to be aware of! As mentioned at the start of this section, my first experience of beginner's mind in any area is almost always frustration. This "defensive" beginner's mind is not open; it is closed. We naturally dislike being a beginner and not knowing. It is natural to be impatient and self-critical in ways that do not help. It can also lead to not talking to others about what we are feeling. To get out of this trap it is useful to remind ourselves that we are at the beginning, to relax and begin practicing. When I do, I always learn in ways that are useful, gratifying, and surprising.

Mastery moves forward in fits and starts. In my yoga, I would begin a new, more advanced practice, having no idea where the practice was taking me. Still, I practiced it every day. I dislike the beginning of new practices. They are awkward and uncomfortable. I don't know what I am doing. I have to think about each step to do the practice. This is beginner's mind. I keep practicing, and practicing becomes less and less uncomfortable. Eventually, the practice becomes a "home," a very comfortable place to be. Then, I often have an insight into where the practice has been taking me. With the insight comes a renewed vigor to my practice. Months later, in many cases, I arrive at the next level of competent practice. I am always glad to be at a new level. There is so much to explore and discover.

When I was 41, I committed myself to using the basic tools all the time, in every aspect of my life. To practice, at first, always requires the use of my mind. I had to think about what I am practicing. I had to keep it before my mind. I had to think about it all the time. The more I practice, the less I have to think about it.

Finally, I practice without thought. The beginning of mastery is to make practice a habit.

Practice: Making it a habit

Mastery is not possible without rigorous practice. Everyone's masterful practice, of anything substantial, goes through exhilarating highs, dull lulls, and uncomfortable doubts ("Am I ever going to learn this?"). Another key to masterful practice is perseverance. Practice when you are scheduled, no matter how you feel.

The great news is that there is always more to discover, learn, and master. As our awareness broadens and deepens, the nuance of our understanding and our behavior is refined. Delightful surprises arise.

Kobe Bryant and Michael Jordan were famous for their rigorous practice ethics. The great ballet dancers of my youth, Suzanne Farrell and Edward Villela, were hailed for their rigorous practice ethics. Classical concert soloists practice five to six hours a day. J. S. Bach worked on his music 10 hours a day, 7 days a week.

Practice leads to improvement. Practice also leads to performance breakthroughs when new skills are mastered. Practice is enhanced by self-reflection and the reflection of others. This does not mean that one cannot make swift progress when starting something new; in fact, often merely starting to practice a new behavior can be hugely beneficial. However, practice is the essence of real mastery of techniques. The habits of applying techniques, learning, and trying again are what drive long-term benefits.

Many things mentioned in this book can be practiced: summarizing, asking others to summarize, asking questions, coupling your facts and opinions. Each of these gets easier over time.

A key question, however, is: Where to start?

The basic communication tools are, at first, counterintuitive.

Our behavioral habits are not to summarize, inquire, or couple facts and opinions when advocating.

I began my mastery of the basic tools by practicing summarizing.

- Every day for about five months, I woke up and immediately reminded myself that I was practicing summarizing and I needed to keep that in my mind's eye all day.

- Of course, as with any other form of meditation, I went in and out of my remembering to summarize.

- I practiced until I found myself summarizing without thinking about it.

- At first the summaries were just for myself and on paper, but I progressed to using them in meetings.

This one behavior often changed the dynamics of an interaction in a positive way, and this encouraged me to go further, first with inquiring, then advocating by coupling facts and opinions.

The key to each "practice" was to have it front and center and to reflect on how it was affecting my conversations. Making it playful also helped. I loved inquiring, for example. I find it so much fun. When my wife and I were still going to parties, I played a game. I tried to get through the party without ever talking about myself. I did this by asking question after question of whoever I was talking with.

Even if it is initially difficult to try some things in a real conversation, practice in private is possible. For example, you can role-play difficult conversations. Record the role-play. Listen to the recording. Note how often you summarize, inquire, and couple your facts and opinions. Practice putting on your defensive body, then replacing it with your competent body. Do this until your body's transitions from defensive to competent occur without your thinking about it.

In front of an analog clock, practice exhaling for twice as long as you inhale. Build this practice up to an hour. In front of a mirror hold your smile. Continue to practice smiling until your smile becomes home. Each of these practices goes deeper in building your awareness of yourself and others in communication. Many will also directly affect your confidence and bearing in difficult situations.

It is probably counterproductive (and too time intensive) to begin trying to build a regular practice for many things at once; select one or two techniques you find very relevant and start with these. Make them second nature over time, note their effects, and then select more techniques. Then add another set of practices.

In Practice

1. Look back at some of the techniques in the previous chapters and select one or two practices which seem most valuable to you. Try to apply them consciously in each relevant meeting, or reflect on how this aspect went each day.

2. If you are unsure of where to start, consider starting with some of the awareness practices. These are often in the "In Practice" section and suggest noting down how different people in meetings react to you and to each other. Note down these behaviors and then extend this to inquiry into what you think needs to be done to improve the dynamics of these meetings.

THE VOICE: THE INVISIBLE FORCE THAT TOUCHES ALL WHO HEAR

Voice is a powerful instrument. Voice can help or hinder our cause. We can sound confused, confident, embarrassed, annoyed, angry, scared, respectful, loving, empathic…the list goes on. Our voice expresses our emotions, and we remain unaware of how our voice is expressing our emotions and influencing others. We seldom hear our own voice in the moment.

We have a set of voices. Each emotional experience has a unique voice. It is a wonderful asset to know the voice of your prominent emotional experiences, to know the influence of your voice, both intended and unintended. Listen to recordings of yourself during meetings. This is part of an efficient and robust way to learn about our voices, to recognize our voice-in-the-moment, to discover the impact of our various voices on others in various situations. With all of this information in hand, we are in the position to choose the voice we want to speak with, in various situations and emotional experiences.

One way to parse voice is by tone, tempo, rhythm, and volume. Some examples follow:

When my client, Bob, talked about himself, he spoke in a slow monotone, a single unvarying tone. Between each word was a moment of silence. Listening to him made me sleepy. When he was in a discussion about difficult problems, his voice was melodic, his rhythm uplifting and lively. His voice invited me to pay attention.

The voice of another client, Joan, was a lovely mezzo soprano. She spoke melodically. The slower she spoke, the funnier she got; her rhythm varied minute to minute. When she expressed anger or upset, she spoke even more slowly, with some melody, her voice louder than usual.

Ann spoke almost in a whisper. She was hard to hear. She spoke very rapidly, with a gentle melody and rhythm. She learned to speak slowly. She learned to raise her volume so she could be heard clearly across a conference room table. Everyone she worked with was grateful for her change in voice.

Jake's voice was baritone. When he was relaxed, and calm, it had a beautiful lilting melody, a comfortable, relaxed rhythm, easy to hear but not too loud. When he was anxious his volume went up, his baritone became piercing and unpleasant to the ear. His tempo was faster. He was hard to listen to.

My own angry voice is loud, my tempo is slow, my rhythm is punchy, I punch each verb louder. My loving voice has a sweet lilt to it, my tone is soft and gentle, my tempo is slow, my rhythm is swaying gently, my volume low, but loud enough to be heard.

A client, Sara, sent me an email thread of several messages and asked me what she should do. I read the thread and emailed back, "You need to apologize." She wrote out her apology five times before it really was an apology. Then it took her 90 minutes of role-playing the right words before she could apologize with a voice that sounded sincere. At first her voice was almost a growl, a deep low growl. Her next voice was that of a marine drill sergeant. Finally, she got to the voice she used when apologizing to her children. She decided that was the voice she wanted to apologize with. A day later she called me and said that her apology was accepted and that she was very glad that she apologized. Then she said, "Boy, I needed that whole 90 minutes of role-playing to find the right voice. Thank you."

When giving critical feedback, I try to remember to soften my voice. My rule is: the harder the feedback, the softer my voice. I do not always succeed, but my success rate keeps rising. Years after working with a client, I bumped into him in an airport. He said to me, "You told me truths that I had to look at. But I felt judged by you. It was in your voice."

I deeply admired my client, Ralph. He was smart, kind, and very funny. He was of first-rate character. I talked with him five years after he retired. He said to me, "I am very glad I worked with you, and I am very glad I never had to work with you again." When I had worked with him, my heart was not yet open. My anger was still deeply rooted. It was expressed in my voice. I sounded judgmental. I lacked compassion. My voice was harsh.

My heart is now open much of the time. My voice reflects the new openness of my heart. Although I lapse into defensiveness once in a while, I mostly act with compassion. In compassion there is no judgment. Compassion is expressed in my voice as sweetness. My wife and friends tell me I now have sweetness in my voice.

How can we choose the right words when we are talking? Here are some suggestions: Be descriptive. Share your facts before your opinion. Avoid judgment and judgmental statements. Do not attribute to others either motives or emotions. Invite summary and then inquiry.

At first, listening to recordings of oneself in action during meetings can be discomfiting. Our voices sound very different when we hear them outside of our heads, rather than inside. Once I grew used to my voice coming from the outside, I tried to put myself in the other person's situation and feel how my voice emotionally affects me. I did this over and over.

IN PRACTICE

1. Learn to hear your various voices as they sound to others.
    1. Imagine a situation in which you were very angry. Imagine the situation until it takes over your body.
    2. Record your voice speaking the angriest thing you wanted to say during the conversation.
    3. Listen to the recording.
    4. Feel how your voice impacts your emotions.
    5. Observe where it puts stress in your body.
2. Repeat this exercise with each of your primary voices:
    1. Confident
    2. Defensive
    3. Respectful
    4. Fearful

THE FACE: A WINDOW ONTO OUR SOUL

If the previous section has you wondering how much of a tell-tale your voice is, this section will tell you that that isn't the half of it! Think of someone you know well. Recall that person smiling at you. What does that feel like? Now, imagine the same person frowning at you. What does that feel like?

Oh, the face…The behavior of the face deeply affects all who see it. The face is so complex: the forehead, the eyes and eyelids, the cheeks, the lips, the chin, and the jaws. All our emotions are transmitted through the face. Elements of the face often communicate our conflicting emotions. The eyes might look scared while the mouth and cheeks are smiling.

Each emotional experience has its own face, similar to the voice. Get to know your various faces. Watch recordings of your meetings. Note your faces. Wonder how each of your faces affects others. Get to know your faces from the outside. What do our faces look like from the outside when we are committed and working with people we respect and admire? What do our faces look like when we are communicating with people we neither respect nor admire?

For many years, when I was worried, my wife would ask me if I was angry with her. She described my face. My eyes had turned into slits. My mouth was pursed, my lips were held tightly, withdrawn from the edges to the center of my mouth. My jaws were bulging, tightly held. My cheeks were tense and unsmiling. Over time, I learned to hold a smile when worrying, and my wife stopped asking if I was angry with her.

I have found it useful to know my face from the inside out. I know what my frown feels like from the inside. My brow is furrowed. My eyes are slits, my lips tightly pursed, my chin shaking with tension. When I hold my frown long enough, my temples start to ache.

My smile: There is a warm glow around my eyes. The tops of my cheeks feel comfortably warm from holding my cheeks in a smile. There is a warmth that rises from my throat and travels to and through my chin and jaws, then up to my eyes, ears, and head.

Videoconferencing has dramatically changed everyone's focus. Sitting around a conference table, we are not focused on each person's face. We see the face from some distance. You notice posture and movements along with facial expressions, and, of course, voice.

Videoconferencing, all we see is faces. Faces have become a much more important communication tool, for good and bad. Most of my clients are unaware of their faces. When thinking, some frown and are unaware of frowning. Some clients always smile and are unaware of always smiling.

Get to know your face from both the inside and outside. Discover what you look like to others. "When the inside of my face feels like this, the outside looks like that." Sit in front of a mirror or a video camera. Close your eyes and think about someone you love. Stay with this until your love has taken over your whole body, including your face. Then open your eyes, staying in your love body. Describe your face. What is the tilt of your head? What is going on with your forehead, your eyes, your cheeks, your lips, mouth, jaw, and ears?

Do the same exercise to discover your angry face, your hurt face, your scared face, your "I am curious" face. For clients who frown, I recommend sitting in front of a mirror and holding a smile. Practice until smiling becomes second nature. For clients who smile, I recommend sitting in front of a mirror and holding a straight face. Discover where your smile starts. Mine starts high in my cheeks. Many report that when they are not smiling, they feel as if something is, or will go, wrong. Many reported feeling free of worry when smiling.

When I videoconference one-on-one with my clients who frown and scowl, I let them know each time they fall into a scowl or frown. Each time they smile, I acknowledge and celebrate the smile. I remind them to put their smile on. I do this while discussing their work issues.

There is an interesting difference in facial expression between basketball players and ice skaters. When Michael Jordan and Kobe Bryant drove to the basket, their tongues were stuck out, their faces contorted. The faces of figure skaters are always serene, no matter how difficult the move they are making. Of course, you never see their tongues, just serene smiles.

In her autobiography Suzanne Farrell tells the story of her first time on stage with the NYCB and how she was standing on stage at the end of the performance, panting (because 2 minutes on stage is quite a workout), and Melissa Hayden told her to control her breathing so nobody would see it, and she never panted like that on stage again. A friend's ballet teacher told her that when she took a class with Melissa Hayden, she said, "I don't want to see your back," meaning always be conscious of what the body is communicating to the audience.

The feelings transmitted by our faces may feel like something to be wary or careful of. This is indeed true in some circumstances, but faces are often a powerful ally in getting information across and expressing feelings. Holding genuine emotions connected to the statements you make will mean your face supports the intent of your words.

IN PRACTICE

1. Practice holding a smile in public. Note how the public responds to you when you are smiling. Compare this with how the public responds to you when you are not smiling.

2. Practice holding a smile when you talk. Note how the listeners respond to you when you smile while talking. Compare this with how listeners respond to you when you are talking without smiling.

3. Try the exercise described in the "Compassion" section of Part IV, thinking about people you love and the feelings they induce.

4. Try the same exercise with someone you have trouble

speaking to or dislike interacting with. How is this different?

5. If you use a video call application, try looking at the recording of a call with the sound off. What do the faces tell you about communications?

6. Get in the habit of having the video call application show the faces of speakers on screen.

Posture and breath: Modulating mood and the nervous system

A man was giving feedback during a team feedback process. He was leaning forward. His right elbow was on the table, the index finger and thumb of his right hand were cocked like a gun, which he fired at the person he was giving feedback to. His feedback was insightful, but it was hurtful in tone.

I interrupted him. I had him sit back with the top of his back on the back of the chair. I told him to keep his hands on his lap. I suggested that he give whatever feedback he was going to give from this posture. He maintained this laid-back posture throughout the discussion. He was still insightful, but his tone was no longer hurtful.

In India, during meetings, I found that women managers, even when they were the highest ranking manager in the room, slouched in the very back of their chairs, looked down, and avoided eye contact. I had them practice sitting at the edge of their chairs, elbows on the table, posture erect. I had them practice looking their colleagues in the eye. Several women managers began to practice by looking their husbands in the eye, for longer and longer periods.

In meetings, I cued them to hold their postures at the edge of their chairs, and to look people in the eye during meetings. The men in the room started paying closer attention to the women in the room. Three months later, most of the women I worked with reported significantly more self-confidence.

Leaning forward increases stress in the moment, thus lowering available awareness, intelligence, competence, and memory. Leaning back, with shoulders relaxed, reduces stress, thus increasing available awareness, intelligence, competence, and memory, in the moment. When videoconferencing, more clients are leaning forward, resting on their elbows. As just mentioned, above, this posture builds stress across the shoulders and up the neck. A remedy is to sit back with the top of the back on the back of their chairs, chest and shoulders relaxed.

It is powerful to take at least a five-minute break every hour. It is energizing to stretch the hands, arms, shoulder, and lower back.

Just as with posture, our breath has a profound effect on our mental and physical state. Breath is simple to talk about, hard to practice, and very powerful. Much of the effect that breath has can be captured in several deceptively simple statements:

- A breath that has a longer inhale and shorter exhale excites the nervous system.

- A breath interrupted during inhale or exhale excites the nervous system.

- A breath with a longer exhale than inhale calms the nervous system.

A longer inhale than exhale is accompanied by defensiveness—fight, flight, or freeze. In high-stress meetings, it is easy to find oneself falling into a defensive pattern, especially when anticipating the need to say something, make one's own point, or raise an objection of some kind. Our inhale grows longer, our exhale shorter. Our nervous system gets activated and we quickly move out of calm awareness and preparation into an active fight, flight, or freeze mode. This clouds what we say. We say it in a voice that conflicts with our intentions. In a meeting it can be very hard to calm down; being conscious of the effect of the breath is already a good start.

In the long run, this comes down to practice; and I recommend practicing breathing to an analog clock with a second hand. Breathe in for five seconds. Breathe out for 10 seconds. Start at five minutes. Build up to an hour. Keep practicing until a longer exhale than inhale is your natural way of breathing. When I last practiced breathing with a clock, my inhale was 10 seconds, my exhale was 20. My wife says that my exhale is longer than my inhale even when I am sleeping. This is a foundational competence that enabled deeper calmness and stillness within me.

IN PRACTICE

1. Begin by breathing in two seconds and breathing out four. Start at 5 minutes, or 10. Build up to 20 minutes or even an hour. Building up too fast builds resistance to practice. Resistance is a signal to do less.

2. After practicing for some time: At the end of each inhale and exhale hold the breath for just a moment.

3. Build up to a 10-second inhale and a 20-second exhale. Start wherever and build up to an hour.

FACING OURSELVES: WALKING ALL THE WAY THROUGH THE FIRE

In the middle of my career, I still had an anger problem that I was only a little aware of: I would often express anger that was unwarranted. I remained unaware. Finally, I was challenged by my wife to master my anger. I inquired of my best friends, several of my siblings, and some clients. I requested that each describe events in which I expressed anger inappropriately. Daily I spent a half-hour feeling my way into each event someone described to me. I thought about the event until it took over my body. I experienced shame, guilt, and embarrassment. I let these feelings take over my body while I focused on visualizing my angry behavior

Several months later, I was driving somewhere. Someone in front of me did something stupid that scared me. I was puffing myself up, getting ready to honk my horn and give the finger. As my anger arose within me, so did my newly cultivated fear of my anger. I watched my fear of my anger take the sharp end of a pin and prick my anger's balloon. I had successfully associated my anger with my shame, guilt, and embarrassment. This interrupted my anger.

Awareness is fine in theory, but it is often hard to know what to be aware of. It often takes extreme incidents and unexpected experiences to draw attention to where it is needed. Sometimes descriptive feedback from others will motivate us to greater awareness. It is also a lifelong process to observe oneself in action. Once you know what to look for, you still have to look. It is all too easy to lapse in attention and let old habits take hold again.

IN PRACTICE

1. Think back to some of the most challenging and difficult incidents you have lived through. Which shone a light on part of your behavior? Did you learn any lessons? Which of the behaviors has recurred since then?

2. Do the same with pleasant experiences: new challenges overcome, a big achievement etc. What were the behaviors that made these things happen? Did the realization change behavior from then on?

Meditation to go deeper: Making awareness, intelligence, and competence more Available

A client in Bangalore prayed for five minutes every morning. He met me because he wanted to be free of his fear of his boss. He told me that he prayed to make no mistakes at work. I suggested that he incrementally build his prayer practice from 5 minutes to 30 minutes. I also suggested that, rather than praying to make no mistakes, he pray for insight into his own fear and the anger of his boss. I suggested that he observe his own fear and learn to separate his fear from his boss's anger.

Six months later he was praying 45 minutes every day. He said he had never imagined the powerful relationship between prayer and rational thought. He was much less often afraid of his boss. His fear was of lower intensity and shorter duration, he was thinking more clearly, and solutions were coming to him more quickly. Then he told me that the only thing that had bothered him about his wife was her aloofness. His wife had meditated at least an hour a day since he first met her. "Now," he said, "I see that she had cultivated nonattachment and equanimity, not aloofness."

There is a direct correlation between stress and defensiveness. The more stressed we are, the stronger our defensive instincts, the harder it is to be sufficiently aware, related, and compassionate, or to apply any of the techniques mentioned in this book. The lower our stress, the less difficult it is to be aware, related, and compassionate and to proceed thoughtfully when communicating.

Meditation, with sufficient practice, lowers the ceiling on our stress and defensiveness. It reduces the frequency, duration, and intensity of our defensive moments. With lower stress, we see more of our field of responsibility. We anticipate problems sooner. Useful solutions come faster.

I interviewed seven friends who all have advanced meditation practices. Each said that an important early milestone was the discovery that their internal voices were not reality. Each level of meditation mastery includes lowering the volume on one's internal voices. With sufficient practice, voices can be turned off. In my own experience, each time I turn off a voice, another, a quieter voice emerges.

The use of a prayer example here may be a surprise. However, there are many forms of meditation, each with its own way of taking the meditator's mind away from the rush of the things pressing on the mind and focusing it on either nothing or a few important questions. Choose a form of meditation that works for you; just ensure that it has the following key elements:

- Regularity of practice so it becomes part of your life

- Quiet internal reflection on emotions, thoughts, and the state of the mind

Many find that having a community to meditate with is very helpful. There are many excellent schools and styles of meditating. Pick a community you feel safe in. Pick a community that is kind and not dogmatic.

Avoid being a dilettante. Power is in the deep mastery of a practice. Choose a practice that is easy for you to return to daily.

An Early Essential Milestone Is Establishing a Regular Practice

Start a regular practice at whatever level you can sustain. Perhaps it is 5 minutes, or 10 minutes. Start where you can and build from there. I have a friend who used a meditation app and practiced 20 minutes a day. I saw him six months after he started. He had grown significantly less anxious. He was easier to be with. He listened better than he had. Two years later he was back to his old anxious manners. He had stopped practicing regularly.

Whenever you find yourself resisting practice, cut back a little. Often, I have taken up a new practice and become too ambitious.

I commit myself to doing the new practice 40 reps instead of 30. Then I find myself dreading the practice, so I cut my reps back to 30 and my dread is gone. About two months into my own yoga practice, I committed myself to practice every day. I made a rule for myself: I could not go to bed until I had done my daily practice.

IN PRACTICE

1. If you are new to meditation, or if it seems a little uncomfortably mystical to you, rather than jump right in, you can start by reserving some other non-structured contemplative time. A good way to do this is to reserve 15–30 minutes for a walk on each day you can spare it. Before you set off, note one or two topics that are bothering you and let them bounce around in your head as you walk. You may not have the solution when you return but you may well have a new perspective or two.

2. If you are just getting started, then consider finding a group or using a book or app. Some guidance really adds motivation early on. The most important thing is simply to start however you can and build up a practice, no matter how little it is per day.

COACHING AND PROMPTING: AN EXTERNAL VIEW ON PROGRESS

In business, teams typically have managers, but they rarely have coaches. Managers are driven to achieve a particular result and are in many ways part of the team. Some managers are also excellent coaches, but this is rare. A coach's role is not to set a vision or drive to a particular goal, but to help teams meld to achieve whatever has been set as the goal. This is a subtle but important difference.

Many of the examples in this book come from times when I coached or was coached. Very often the smallest insight can change a deeply held attitude or unlock new potential. At one point I said to a client who owned an architecture firm with his wife, "You need to stop interrupting your wife and listen to her. She is smarter than you are." Thirty years later, this client said to me, "Your feedback saved my marriage before it reached a crisis."

Teams who want to be free of defensiveness need the assistance of an external consultant who is not defensive and has experience helping teams overcome their defensiveness.

With luck, you will have access to professional coaches for yourself or your team (and it is worth seeking these out). In this section we cover some of the techniques which you should seek out and, in the absence of a coach, consider applying yourself with your teams.

What does a good coach focus on?

There are many styles and schools of coaching. Most accommodate and enable the defensive routines of their clients. This approach by coaches, of treating the client's defensive routines as taboo, is unfortunately prevalent. When a coach treats the client's defensive routines as taboo, problems associated with these defensive routines cannot be addressed or resolved. While this style of coaching may help clients feel better, it rarely helps improve behavior or performance.

I favor schools of coaching that address a client's defensive routines. At first, this requires courage. Addressing defensiveness directly requires raising taboo issues. Relatedness is required. It is essential that coaches avoid putting their own interests above their clients' interests. During the first twenty-some years of my consulting and coaching career, I lacked compassion and still enjoyed lots of success. Since I cultivated compassion, all my experience, professional and personal, is much more deeply gratifying.

How to qualify a coach

The best way to qualify a coach is to work on a challenging, important problem with the potential coach, one that you feel some defensiveness about. After you have done the work with the potential coach, ask yourself the following questions: What did the coach tell me about myself? Did the coach surprise me with insight? Did the coach help me see ways in which I was part of the problem that I was unaware of? How did I feel working with the coach? Is this something I would like to do again? This is a powerful way of qualifying a coach.

You can learn from interviewing the coach's past clients. Ask them: How did the coach add value? What did you learn about yourself? What habits did the coach help you become aware of and change? How did the coach do this? What do you wish the coach had done differently?

IN PRACTICE

1. If there are coaches available to you or your team, who do they focus on: individuals or the team as a whole? Do they sit in on team meetings? If not, consider asking them to attend one or two.

2. If there are no coaches available, who on the team could play an observer role in meetings and raise awareness of how communication is flowing?

3. If you are a team manager, which of the communication behaviors could you begin to coach your team on by setting an example?

Assessing your team

Assessing your team's culture can be a good step in motivating your team to commit themselves to mastery of the tools described in this handbook. The assessment searches for your team's defensive errors and will help your team identify what improvements it wants to develop next. The challenge is raising and discussing your assessment of the team with the team.

Every team produces issues that need to be managed better but are systematically avoided. Look for the issues that are discussed passionately in private and are avoided in the appropriate forums. To discover important off-limits issues, talk with individuals one-on-one. When you talk to more than one teammate at a time, the team's unspoken defensive rules govern what is and is not said. Team discussions of their defensiveness can be exhilarating when facilitated well. They can be harmful if the discussion is defensive.

The team assessment section repeats the list of the most common errors of defensiveness and turns them into a set of questions to consider. The Common Defensive Team Errors are:

1. Issues that need to be better managed remain undiscussed in appropriate forums.
2. Important problems remain after more than one effort to resolve them.
3. Poor performance remains unaddressed and unimproved.
4. Some communication is problematic.
5. Decisions are not made.
6. There is competition for influence, opportunities, and resources.
7. Unresolved disagreements are blockers.

Knowing these errors, we can formulate a set of questions to ask about a team's communication:

1. What issues are addressed in timely and satisfactory ways?

What is the value?

2. What issues are not addressed in a timely and satisfactory way? What is the cost to the team?

3. What issues need to be managed better yet remain undiscussed? What is the cost to the team?

4. What would happen to a teammate who raised these issues in the appropriate forums?

5. Whose performance, of what, has remained unimproved for too long?

6. Who is responsible for making sure this poor performance is improved satisfactorily?

7. What would happen to a teammate who raised the performance issues in the appropriate forum?

8. Where, and between whom, is miscommunication a recurring problem? What is the cost to the team?

9. Which tasks take too long? What is the cost to the team?

10. Who is excluded from influencing decisions important to them?

11. What disagreements, among whom, need to be resolved to get something important done? What is the cost to the team?

12. Who is responsible for making sure each disagreement is satisfactorily resolved?

13. What would happen to a teammate who told the responsible person it was time to resolve the disagreements?

It may be that these questions already highlight a few key areas to work on and provide enough of a focus to begin with. Over time, however, it can also be beneficial to visualize where a team sits against a hierarchy of communication. There are potentially many ways of expressing what is better or worse, but a simple model I have found useful is as follows:

1. Important tasks do not get done.

2. Important tasks get done, but not to acceptable timeliness, quality, or performance.

3. Everything gets done, but the culture is defensive (see the Common Symptoms of Defensiveness):

4. The leader is held accountable by the team. All important issues are raised on time, discussed with sufficient specificity, and resolved satisfactorily.

5. Teammates hold each other accountable, in the moment, and over time.

6. Doing 4 and 5 with compassion.

7. Doing 4 and 5 with compassion, humor, and playfulness.

These levels are not necessarily exclusive. It's possible that in some areas, things are getting done and there is even adequate feedback or discussion, while in other areas there are important taboo subjects that stop all communication. While it often takes time to improve in all areas, difficult communications in one area can degrade trust and, hence, communication, across the board.

As a result, if you find yourself with wildly different scores across different areas the team works on, try to use the strength in some areas to address the situation in others.

Teams I have used this level assessment with have often been initially shocked at finding they score poorly in some areas or that some team members score the team much lower than others. The reason is that we are so used to our communication environment and are only dimly aware that it could be better. The assessment can provide a useful rallying point for identifying and improving issues.

PART VII

Conclusion: A lifelong journey

As humans, we experience some of our greatest joys through communication and suffer some of our greatest pain. At work, our experience can range from a great feeling of progress in a meeting to a deep sense of dread at having to talk to someone about a difficult issue that up until now has been systematically avoided.

It is easy to imagine these experiences are just part of how the world is and to be accepted, accepting that unpleasant communications are a fact of life.

My hope is that this book has helped persuade you that that's not always the case. There are reasons for the way we and others communicate; becoming aware of them can make a tremendous difference! The hidden drivers behind communication are so often invisible to us that even a little progress can help a lot:

- Defensiveness is ubiquitous in our communications and often not visible to us—or if it is visible, it is not discussable. Our instinct drives us to keep things back, say things we don't mean, and hide our true feelings. In teams, it leads to misunderstandings, mistrust, and the drawing of battle lines where none should be.

- Awareness of our own defensiveness and that of others unlocks this puzzle. Knowing why we or others are driven to react in a certain way and pausing to decide whether this is really what we should say have tremendous benefits.

- This growing awareness is the stepping-stone to improvements in trust, courage, relatedness, and the other positive qualities described in the book. Each of these qualities brings us more positive results from communication and deepens our bond with others.

I hope the techniques in this book—from simpler practices such as summarizing and practicing our own listening to the deeper factors such as awareness—will help you make your communication experience more of a joy than a pain over time.

There is no magic bullet for every situation, and mastery of communication is a lifelong journey that is never complete. However, the steps along the way can all help make communication more joyful.

Thinking back to my meeting with Jed in Harvard square, it's deeply touching to me that his one act of telling me something he thought might benefit me influenced my life so deeply. Years later, when I met him again, he had no recollection of what he had done. It just goes to show that when you are thoughtful in the moment, it can have a big effect on someone, even if it doesn't register deeply for yourself.

I wish you a wonderful journey in better team communication!

Los Angeles, Spring 2020 to Summer 2022

BIBLIOGRAPHY

Argyris, Chris (1962) *Interpersonal Competence and Organizational Effectiveness.* Homewood, Ill: Dorsey Press.

Argyris, Chris (1971) *Management and Organizational Development.* New York: McGraw-Hill

Argyris, Chris and Schon, Donald (1978) *Organizational Learning: A Theory of Action Perspective.* Reading, PA: Addison-Wesley

Bion, Wilfrid (1961) *Experiences in Groups: and other Papers.* London: Routledge.

Caro, Robert (2003) *Master of the Senate: The Years of Lyndon Johnson.*

Chernow, Ron (1990) *The House of Morgan.* New York: Grove Press.

Chernow, Ron (1998) *Titan: the Life of John D. Rockefeller, Sr.* New York: Vintage Books

Flexner, James, Thomas (1967) *George Washington in the American Revolution 1775 – 1783.* New York: Little Brown

Hibbert, Christopher (1997) *Wellington: A Personal History.* Reading, PA: Perseus Books

Hirschman, Albert, O. (1970) *Exit, Voice, and Loyalty.* Cambridge: Harvard University Press

Salzberg, Sharon, (2018) *Lovingkindness.* Boulder, CO: Shambala Publications

Schon, Donald (1983) *The Reflective Practitioner.* New York: Basic Books

INDEX

ABOUT THE AUTHOR

I have an EdM from Harvard University and an MS and PhD from the Anderson School of Management at UCLA. My consulting career began at Hughes Aircraft Company, a very important defense contractor until General Motors acquired it in the late 1980s. Over the first 11 years of my career, I consulted to every corner of Hughes. I worked with teams brewing gallium arsenide, designing chips, subsystems, and major systems: radar, satellite navigation, surface ships, and electro-optical data systems. I learned how outstanding research was done and managed, what excellent product development and product management looked like. I learned to improve the communication and performance of all kinds of teams. In the 40 years since then I have consulted to high tech on both the engineering and marketing sides, biotech on the science side, financial services, and a few firms in law, architecture, and political consulting.

Made in the USA
Columbia, SC
19 February 2023

12534825R00113